To Life

A Holocaust Survivor's Journey to Freedom

WRITTEN BY **MARSHA COOK**
AS TOLD BY **SALA LEWIS**

© Copyright 2012, Marsha Casper Cook

All Rights Reserved.

No part of this book may be reproduced, stored in a retrieval system, or transmitted by any means, electronic, mechanical, photocopying, recording, or otherwise, without written permission from the author.

ISBN: 978-1-60414-582-3

Aknowledgments

I would like to thank my family, friends and clients, for supporting me in my endeavors. It has always meant quite a lot to me that you knew I could do this. And to Sala, I thank you for sharing your story with me and for teaching me the true meaning of courage.

Preface

I was only ten years old when this all began, losing all the innocence of youth but gaining strength with each breath. After all the evidence that exists there are those who feel the Holocaust never existed. I hope in my lifetime I will never have to face anyone who tells me it didn't happen. It's certainly unbelievable what a person goes through. Who can explain or even try to understand why I am here to tell my story and millions of others are not?

I have been taking on speaking engagements, difficult as they are for me, to help all of us who have suffered through the tragic events of the Holocaust. As a member of the last generation to have gone through the Holocaust, I feel an obligation to expose the truth for what it was. Don't my parents, brothers, sisters, aunts and uncles deserve at least this much?

As I have stood before strangers and opened my heart to them, I feel a sense of accomplishment. I don't use notes and I don't prepare speeches. What I speak are the words of truth that are in my heart and can never be erased, even by time.

There is nothing stronger than a person or weaker than a person. We may be tested many times over and we may at some times want to give up, but when we are pushed against a wall and forced to make that choice, each time we must choose life.

"TO LIFE....L'CHAIM....

To Life

The question is to be curious
To be curious is to care
To care is to love
To love is to forget
But if we forget
Who will answer the questions
Who will be there
To make sure
The deaths of our loved ones
Will have not have been in vain,
So please don't ask us to forget
The pain and the sadness
The outburst and
The tears
They belong to us
They are dreams,

They are the sparks of light
That survive in us
To remind us
Of love and honor
And of being who we are
We have been spared by G-d
To hold in our hearts
All that is dear to us,
For we as a people have
Survived
We are not just Jews
We represent honor
And courage

We are the inspiration
We represent love,
We are not only survivors
We are teachers
We are friends
We are the assurance that
The Holocaust did happen
We are here to repeat
The facts
So it can't happen again,
Yes, we are the reminders
But you my children
You are the future
You have the power
To say no
We didn't ...

In the Beginning

I was ten years old when the Germans separated my family. It happened so quickly we didn't even get to say goodbye. We lived in Sosnowicz, Poland, and all we were told was the Germans needed workers. There were no choices. When the Germans came to get you, you went. If you didn't go, you were killed. That was the beginning of the end.

I never dreamt that I'd never see my family again. It wasn't supposed to happen that way. My parents were going to grow old together. We were going to share our lives together, the good times, the bad times and everything in between. Then in a flash, everything changed.

The Germans took my family away from me, one by one. I never quite understood why, but they told me it was because we were Jewish. I was taught not to question, so I didn't.

Then the day came, the final separation. I had gone out to play for a short while but when I returned, I came home to an apartment that had been sealed off and I wasn't allowed in.

I never did see the inside of that apartment again, but I can still remember the joy we shared every evening at dinnertime. We sang songs and told jokes. Sometimes we didn't sing that well or tell terribly funny jokes, but we had each other. That was the feeling I liked best.

Salucia was my birth name but everyone called me Sala, the name I prefer.

I was born on a snowy, cold Christmas day. My father, Simon, was a

Marsha Casper Cook/as told by Sala Lewis

butcher and my mother, Eve, was a wonderful homemaker. I was one of eight children - three girls and five boys – Karl, Phillip, David, Kamek, Hanusz, Toby and Dora. Dora was the light of my life, and as the years passed she was the one who got me through it all. Without her, I never would have survived. She was my lucky penny.

The Loneliness

Long ago, I learned never to take anything for granted. That's how I got through the hard parts, especially the loneliness. At the very beginning, they told us the work camps were just places to work, nothing more. When Dora left, she promised she would write, and she did just enough to let us know she was alive. When her letters came, mother was so happy and so was everyone else. We took turns reading the letters over and over again. Usually on those days, dinner was special and mother didn't seem as angry. But then there was the next, and there were no letters. Those were the bad days. The very, very bad days.

As the days passed, I missed Dora so much more than I thought I would. There was nothing very different about our relationship. We were sisters. We fought a little, yelled a bit and sometimes we even had fistfights. We were rather ordinary, so I guess it was normal to miss even those fights. And I did.

We lived in a very small apartment, which even in the best of circumstances made for some pretty rough times. But all and all, I think we all started to miss the squabbles and the "he said this," and "she said that" after Karl, Phillip and David left for the work camps.

Our family was getting smaller, and day by day, my mother and father were growing older. They didn't say much, and maybe that was part of the problem. The Gestapo came, they took and we suffered, but we didn't talk about it.

Every night at the dinner table, our conversation was less and less. In fact, what used to be such a special time of the day became my least favorite. Sometimes I pretended to have a stomachache, just so I wouldn't have to sit there and look at the empty chairs.

Late at night, I used to lay awake and think about the good times. There was one particular evening that was right up there with the best of the memorable times. It was Chanukah.

Mother had just brought the last batch of latkes to the table. Phillip looked at David, Dora looked at me and we all looked at Karl, hoping he would get the message. In a minute or two, we knew our message had been well received. Karl walked over to the gramophone and looked at Mother. She could read his mind as well as any one of us. She nodded to Karl and he turned on the music. One by one, we all got up to dance and sing, all except Father. He just watched.

Then, as always, Mother grabbed his hand and tried to get him up to dance. Usually he said no, but not that night. That night he danced. I watched Mother and Father holding each other tightly as they danced, hoping someday to have someone love me the way my father loved my mother.

I overheard my father as he whispered to my mother, "Eva my dear, we may never be rich but look ... look at our children. This is what we posses. No man could ever want more."

The next night, the Gestapo came. That was only the first visit. There would be many others to follow, as well as reminders of what each day might bring. It was the constant fear of the visits that upset my father the most, especially the night before Dora left for the work camp.

I can still feel the pain as I remind myself of Dora's last night at home. My family thought I was sleeping, but after overhearing their conversation, I didn't sleep a wink.

My father watched as Dora packed a small bag. "When you come back my child, I will not be here," he said. "So you go tomorrow and remember to do whatever you have to to stay alive. I promise you life will offer you more, much more, but never give up what you believe in. Never."

Dora's voice quivered as she spoke. "Don't say that. You will be here when I return. I know you'll be here. You just have to."

"Dora, listen to me," my father said. "I've had my life. When I stand back and take a good look at all my children, I can ask for no more. I have no right."

"You have every right," Dora said, as she put her arms around Father and gave him a great big hug. "Of course, you have every right, we are family. We belong together, and we will be together again. G-d will have it no other way."

All night I tossed and turned, wondering why I wanted so much more than anyone else. My dreams were of acting and performing on stage. What if the Gestapo took me? I wouldn't go. I would tell them no way and ask them to go. Why didn't Dora do that? She should have done that.

As the days and nights passed, our entire community of Jewish friends was slowly being taken away. It was a slow process with quite an effect on everyone. Father didn't smile as much as he used to and Mother kept herself busy. She cooked and cleaned and cleaned and cooked, and when she heard bad news, she cleaned some more.

We didn't talk about what was happening, but it was quite evident to me we were no longer the happy family we used to be. Every time I looked into my father's eyes, they were red and swollen. I knew he had been crying, but he never admitted to it. It was becoming more difficult to pretend our situation wasn't critical, but as long as my family pretended, so did I. I had become very good at pretending. We all had.

Days would pass without changes. However, when my older brother Karl's wife Lusia and their son Jurek came to live with us, things did change. Father talked a bit more and Mother sometimes even smiled. Having a baby in the house eased the tension a bit for us, but not for Lusia. Every day we waited for the mailman, hoping to hear from Karl, but there were no letters. There were never going to be any letters.

As if enough hadn't happened, Lusia had gone out to get some milk and never returned. After three hours of pacing back and forth at the window, my father went out to see if he could get anyone to tell him what happened. We knew it was getting worse.

When he finally did return and my mother saw the look on my father's face, she cried out to him, "They took her. The Gestapo, they took her. Oh my G-d."

It was horrible watching little Jurek standing at the door, waiting for his

Marsha Casper Cook/as told by Sala Lewis

mother to come home. It was days later when we finally found out Lusia wouldn't be coming back. That's when I began to write letters to myself. I needed to feel as if I was doing something that mattered.

Letter To Me —

Maybe if I were a little older or a little smarter, I would understand just what was happening. Sometimes late at night when everyone was sleeping, I would get up and look outside. All I ever saw was darkness. I didn't see the soldiers marching and I couldn't hear the cries. I don't know if it's just the beginning or the very end. Why doesn't someone tell me something?

—Me

Without a Goodbye

It was a day like any other. As I raced up the stairs, I waved goodbye to my friends. When I got to my apartment, I knew something was wrong. Our apartment was sealed off and I couldn't get in. My family was gone and no one knew where they were.

I tried not to panic, but I was scared. I didn't understand what had happened and why they didn't wait for me. I didn't know what to do, so I ran outside and into the street. I knocked on the neighbors' doors, but no one knew what had happened to my family.

Finally, I ran to the schoolyard after someone on the street said my parents would be there. I had to keep wiping my eyes as the tears kept falling from my eyes. When I walked around the back, I could see my mother in the window.

As she waved to me, I moved closer toward the window. I called out to her, "I want to be with you. Take me with you Mother, I'm afraid."

"Salusia, my child," Mother said as she called back to me. "Do not be afraid. I will wait for you up here. But first you must run to your aunt's house and get some money to buy candy for the children."

I looked up at my mother and shouted. "Please don't do this to me. I want to be with you."

"You will," she said, as she called down to me.

"Where's father?" I asked.

Mother shrugged her shoulders and motioned for me to go. As always, I did as she asked. While walking away, I couldn't help but wonder why my younger brother, sister and Jurek were with her but I wasn't. I looked back and waved goodbye.

Mother waved back and said, "I'll be here when you return."

But she wasn't. No one was. That was the last time I ever saw them.

That night I wandered the streets, hoping Father would be out there somewhere. When I got tired, I walked back to our apartment, where I sat on the steps hoping my father would come back to find me. Somebody should have, but nobody did. Instead, I woke up sitting on the stairs alone. I couldn't help but feel abandoned. I was.

Finally, I realized I was on my own. Even my aunts and uncles wouldn't take me in. No one wanted the extra burden. One time, my uncle sent me out some scraps of food to eat, to be eaten outside only. They were afraid I would bring in unwanted germs. The hell with the germs, I thought. What about me? Doesn't anybody realize I'm still a little girl, a scared little girl?

The hours turned into days and the days turned into weeks. I never slept in the same place twice. As I roamed from place to place, I heard bits and pieces about the Germans and the horrible things they were doing to my people, just because we were Jewish. None of it made any sense, but it did make me cry a lot. I tried my best not to think of my family being tortured or worse than that. Word of the death camps left me sleepless and afraid to close my eyes. I tried to have faith in G-d, but sometimes I wondered if there really was a G-d. I was certain if there was one, how could he let this happen? And more than how, why?

Letter To Me –

Maybe if I could have kissed my mother and father goodbye, I wouldn't feel so empty. Maybe if I were with them, I could close my eyes at night and not see their faces. Maybe if I didn't love my brothers and sisters so much, it wouldn't hurt so much not to see them again. Maybe if I would stop crying, I would feel better. Maybe this and maybe that. Maybe if I closed my eyes and pretended I wasn't me, I wouldn't be. Yes, I think I'd like that a lot.

—Me

My Turn

Sometimes I would imagine myself kicking the German Gestapo when it was my turn to go. I thought myself stronger than most and certainly able to defend myself. But when a Nazi soldier holds a gun to your head, you weaken. I certainly did.

Then the inevitable happened. It was my turn. I was part of a large Jewish cleanup. The Nazis took both the young and the not so young. Men, women and children were ordered to march. Despite the pouring rain, we did as they said.

At a distance, I could hear the chanting of other kids. Those that chanted were referred to as Hitler's kids. "Kill the Jews. Kill the Jews. Jews are no good." Even when they weren't calling out to us, I could hear their voices bellowing in my ears.

Everything about that evening will never leave my mind. The Gestapo treated us horribly. We weren't allowed to sit or lie down. We had to stand the entire night. Several times that night, I wanted to scream out at the top of my lungs, "Please dear G-d don't do this to us," but I didn't.

When morning came and the rain stopped, I looked around at all the men, women and children who had made it through the night. I couldn't help but wonder if they were as afraid as I was. We never spoke to each other, but at that moment I knew I might never know their names but would never forget their faces.

Several daylight hours had passed before the Gestapo started to do what was referred to as a roundup, arranging groups depending on age and capabilities to be transported to Auschwitz and Treblinka, the known death camps.

The commotion caused unrest among all of us. Tears were shed and screams were heard. Then all of a sudden, the Gestapo started to randomly shoot at us, especially the young babies. I was sick to my stomach as I watched the Gestapo laugh as they tossed babies into the air and shot them.

A young woman with a small baby nestled in her arms was standing next to me, trying to comfort her baby as he cried. I closed my eyes in prayer, hoping the little baby would stop crying. Then from behind, a German soldier approached the young woman.

The soldier called out to the woman. "Keep that damn baby quiet."

The woman responded with a nod. Then she stroked her son's head as she whispered to him, "Shhh ... please don't cry."

But still the baby cried. I took a deep breath as I watched the soldier reach for the baby and grab him away from his mother. The guard looked at the woman in anger. "Didn't I tell you to shut that damn baby up? Didn't I?"

The woman cried as she held out her hands, trying to get her son back. The Gestapo pulled back, "Get away ... you stupid Jew."

It all happened so fast. The soldier tossed the baby up in the air and nodded to another Gestapo soldier, who then shot the baby in mid-air. Seconds later, after giving one of the most blood-curdling cries I had ever heard, the baby fell to the ground dead. I tearfully watched as the baby's mother fell to her knees, lying over her son's torn-apart body.

Another soldier stood before the woman and kicked her in the belly. "You see Jew, now he's quiet."

As if that wasn't enough, the Gestapo soldier who had shot the baby pointed his gun to the woman's head and fired. I don't know if I will ever be able to stop seeing the woman's blood splatter all over her son's.

What upset me most was the carefree way in which the Gestapo soldiers killed people. How they ever went home at night and kissed their own children will always remain a mystery to me.

Once again, the Gestapo began to count. A woman with slightly graying hair eased toward me and whispered in my ear, "Reach back toward my hand and take my bra. Hurry and put in on, you will look older." Even though I didn't quite understand why, I did exactly as she said.

Luckily, I had just enough time to wiggle the bra from my ankles to my waist, which allowed me to be chosen during the reselection to go to the right. There were only two ways to go, valid to the right, invalid to the left. Useful to the right, useless to the left.

I never got to thank the woman in the line, but she saved my life. Because of her kindness and concern, I was treated as an adult, which prolonged my life. Even though one might think death might outweigh life when faced with such horrible choices, it doesn't. I chose life, and if I had to do it all over again, my choice would always be the same. There is no gift greater than life.

It was obvious to any of us who remained in line that the Gestapo was not there to please us. As luck was with me, I quietly listened to the faults of the others who waited in line for assignment. Begging didn't seem to help, so I waited until it was just the right time to ask for what I wanted. Placement was everything.

"Please let me go where my family is," begged the woman next to me.

"Now why in hell would I do that?" the Gestapo soldier said as he wacked her on the back with his gun.

As I watched the woman suffer as she tried to get up from the ground, I wondered if I would be able to get any satisfaction when it was my time to stand before those horrible Gestapo soldiers - men and women who, with just one motion of their hand, could have us killed or shoot us themselves.

"I would like to be sent where my sister is," I said in a straightforward voice when it was my turn to stand before the jury of horror.

The Gestapo soldier took a second look at me. "Did you see what happened to the woman before you?"

I nodded, realizing the less said the better.

"And you still ask to be sent to your sister," the Gestapo soldier said with certainty.

With courage I quickly responded, "Yes I do."

15

Marsha Casper Cook/as told by Sala Lewis

When the Gestapo soldier motioned for another soldier to come closer, I thought I had pushed a little to hard and would probably end up in Auschwitz or Treblinka. I was shaking inside, but on the outside I was cool as a cucumber.

That's when I reminded myself of my mother's words. "Salucia," she would say, "If you were in a fire, you would not burn."

She was right, because no sooner did I ask to be with Dora then a Gestapo soldier walked over to me. "Consider yourself lucky," he said. "You've got guts." I could still hear him laughing and mumbling to himself as he walked away. "How do you like that, a Jew with guts."

Letter To Me –

I don't know if this horrible feeling in the pit of my stomach will ever go away. I don't know if I will once again be able to laugh, sing or feel loved. I don't know if I'll be able to take a deep breath, smile or enjoy life, but if I do there will never be a day that I won't thank G-d for helping me through this. Please G-d, hear me cry.

—Me

Dora

There were about one hundred of us shoved into the boxcar on one of the trains transporting us to the work camps, or as the Gestapo referred to it, resettlement. After they squeezed the very last one of us in and sealed the doors shut, we were so tired we collapsed. Being cooped up in a dark boxcar with strangers was quite unpleasant, but as with everything else the Gestapo made us do, we said nothing. Fear is horrifying.

It might have been foolish, but I trusted that Dora would be waiting for me. I only hoped the Gestapo soldiers didn't change their mind and not tell me that our destination had changed. Of course, a deception like that was easy for them.

They didn't care if our hopes were up, being Jewish already meant one step into the grave. I didn't know how far we traveled or if we had stopped, because it was easier to sleep than to worry about what came next. However, I do remember the rushes of daylight that blinded my eyes when the doors were finally opened. When I jumped off of the train and felt my feet touch ground, my heart was beating very fast.

At first we were told to march in a line and not to try anything funny. If any one of us got out of line, they threatened to kill every last one of us. No one took the chance of testing them because we knew our lives meant nothing to them, just another dead Jew.

It was very warm that day, almost uncomfortable and very hard to move, let alone march. But I would have marched anywhere for any length of time to be with Dora. From the very moment I walked through those gates, I knew a guardian angel had taken me there.

Dora stood there among the hundreds of others waiting to welcome their friends, neighbors and family. The familiarity of Dora's sweet smile eased my fears. My heart was now beating twice as fast as before, almost until I couldn't breathe. And to think I had almost stopped believing in G-d.

With tears in her eyes, Dora took hold of me. We hugged each other and cried for the longest time, and when we finally did let go of each other, we cried some more. Despite the constant threat of death, I felt safe in Dora's arms.

Then the questions began. Dora wanted answers and I sadly had to inform her of our tragedy.

"So where is everyone?" Dora asked. "Mother, Father, our brothers and sisters. Where, tell me where they have gone?"

I pointed to myself, trying to hold back the tears. "I'm the only one left."

There was terror in Dora's eyes. "I don't understand. What do you mean everyone's gone? This couldn't be. G-d wouldn't do this. No, he couldn't."

"But he did," I angrily shouted back. "I don't know if they're dead or alive. All I know is that there hasn't been word of them for weeks. They're gone, I know they are."

I couldn't say any more. I had hoped Dora would understand that I couldn't talk, at least not then. I assumed she knew, because for the longest time neither of us spoke.

From the moment I entered those gates, Dora took care of me. She was so wonderful. I couldn't believe how my luck had changed. I didn't feel afraid or lonely anymore. Dora was all the family I needed.

Later, there were endless introductions. Dora had made herself quite comfortable at the work camp. The women who shared the same barracks with Dora became her family. She was like a mother to the girls who needed one. She was a friend who they could share their thoughts and concerns with, but most importantly they could trust her. The day my family was taken away from me was the day I lost trust. Regaining those feelings certainly wouldn't be easy.

Later, Dora showered me. Ironically, she sensed my needs and she attended to them. Happily, the green dress I had been wearing for days had been tossed aside. It was replaced by a dress that did not fit, but I felt clean. At this point in time, all I cared about was getting that filthy dress and all that it represented off of me.

"Follow me," Dora said as she walked me over to a long wooden table where I sat down to eat a bowl of soup and a piece of bread. I don't remember what kind of soup was in the bowl or if the bread was stale or fresh, but I remember feeling full.

For the next few days, I was Dora's shadow. Wherever she went I went, and vice versa. Within a very short time, Dora and I were inseparable. I had finally begun to trust again. It was a slow experience, but I was coming along just fine. Naturally, Dora had everything to do with that.

Each night after the lights went out, the silence was unbearable. To help me ease the pain of remembering only terrible things, I tried to recall one of my most pleasant experiences. Remembering was painful, but forgetting would have been far worse.

Mother had always encouraged us to develop our natural talents. Every night after dinner, my brothers and sisters and I would sing and dance. I couldn't wait for the day when I could perform on the stage and be a big Hollywood star. Who knew there would be no tomorrow? Who knew all our dreams would be taken away by a man they called Adolph Hitler? Who knew the worst of the humiliation was yet to come?

Every day after work, Dora would try to encourage my dreams, regardless of how bad a day we had or how much work the Gestapo pushed on us. Dora believed in my dreams and me. She helped me keep that part of my life alive and vital, hoping there would be an end to the terror and hardship we were going through.

I was luckier than most. I had Dora. Even at the workshop, Dora did what she could without getting herself in any trouble to make sure I could carry the workload the Gestapo gave me. After all, I was only a young girl. I was supposed to be strong and able to pull my own weight. Often, Dora would do my work if I got too tired. She was amazing.

I came to rely on Dora for everything, as did many of the women in the work camp. I would hear Dora whisper in their ears, "Do as they say ... this will pass."

There was one night in particular when if I didn't have Dora with me,

I'm not sure I would have survived. I was feeling very low that day. One of the women in our barracks had been taken away in the middle of the night. The Gestapo said it was due to illness, but who knows? The truth was something the Gestapo changed.

I was in bed crying. Dora knelt beside me, stroking my forehead and trying to comfort me.

"Dora, please go back to bed. They'll shoot you or hit you, please," I begged.

Dora whispered. "It's OK, the two women on duty tonight had one too many swigs. They're drunk."

"Are you sure?" I asked.

Dora nodded. "And you are you OK?"

"I guess so," I answered. "But I 'm scared, very scared. Don't you ever get scared?"

"Of course. Everyone here is scared, but what are our choices? We have none. So we do as they say and another day goes by and we're alive, so it's OK."

After that explanation, Dora reassured me that soon we'd be in Hollywood, and of how beautiful the costumes I'd be wearing would be, and how the music would be just right for my entrance on center stage.

Once again, Dora had put my mind at ease and I slept a lot easier. I often wondered if Dora really did sleep when she went back to bed after our talks, or if she did have trouble as I did. When I questioned her she always said yes, but she never really convinced me.

Dora believed in my talents so much, she used to tell everyone about my singing and dancing and how proud she was of me. She promoted me as the child star who could sing like a bird and dance like an angel. And with all her promoting, she did what she set out to do.

The Gestapo women wanted me to entertain them, and in return they would give me extra food. Naturally, the extra food made it very appealing. Extra food meant extra strength for the other women and myself.

The first time it happened was very late at night, almost morning. We were all sleeping, but the guards were drinking and partying. After all, when we worked, they could sleep. They didn't care if we were tired. A tired Jew still worked, and there were absolutely no exceptions.

I was awoken by a firm nudge on my shoulder. "Get up. It's show time. You're stretched out like a herring. We want to see you dance. So get your little ass up and let's begin."

At first I didn't answer.

Again the S.S. woman shouted. "Did you hear me, little one?"

I slowly lifted my head up, only to be summoned by three large Gestapo women. One of the Gestapo yelled out, "We want to be entertained. Get up now."

Dora stood up and answered for me, "She'll be ready in a minute."

With Dora's help, I was ready in less than a minute. Then without much ado, I walked to the center floor of the barracks and began to sing and dance.

Everyone in the barracks was up watching me. As I looked around the room, I saw the faces of the women who in only a few hours would have to be awake and ready to march to work. They made me uncomfortable, but getting extra food for them made it feel appropriate.

From that night on, I had made a place for myself. It wasn't my dream, but if it made it any easier on the women in my barracks, then it was all right with me. My dancing soon became the ultimate in entertainment for the Gestapo women.

It was from my dancing and singing debut that I began my survival training. I was learning to play by the Gestapo's rules, always reminding myself of Dora's repetitive instructions – "Keep your mouth shut and do as they say."

I was not the only one in our barracks who had theatrical experience – there were many others. When the other women realized it would make a difference in our treatment at the work camp, they came forward and performed. Sometimes we performed together, sometimes solo. We also performed entire productions, costumes and all. Our costumes weren't elaborate – mostly ripped sheets and scrapes of material – but we performed well. And yes, we were rewarded with food, which kept some of us a little more energized.

When we danced, we danced without tap shoes and when we sang, sometimes it was without music. Nevertheless, the Gestapo always applauded. Those of us who performed did some of the best acting I've ever seen, and it wasn't only our on-stage performance. It was how we smiled at the Gestapo on the outside and cried on the inside. It was very hard for all of us to enjoy our shows, certainly because to us as Jews, we were only doing whatever we had to for survival.

Our willingness to perform was out of pure desperation. Each of us who performed was given extra food, which we shared with the others in our barrack.

We were not selfish to each other – in fact, we were equal and considerate, certain we were to face hell whenever our time came. We made no mistake why we were there. We were on borrowed time so we lived minute to minute – no more, no less.

On all the days that followed, everything went quite the same. We were awoken at the crack of dawn, fed maybe a bit of soup and bread, and then we marched to the factories. Factories that weren't glamorous, but we did have bathrooms and a place to sit. As far as any other accommodations, there were none.

When it snowed we marched without boots, and when it got warmer we marched without water. When it rained we got soaked, and when push came to shove, we did whatever the Gestapo ordered. They didn't value our lives as we did.

The deafening noise from the large cotton machines we worked on made it impossible to have lengthy conversations, if any at all. We were there to work, not to talk. We had strict instructions not to talk to anyone, especially the Polish workers from the outside world, who worked and then went home. They were instructed never to converse with any of us, and they followed their orders to a tee. The plan ran smoothly and we never found out anything that had happened outside the camp. Amazing but true.

There were times when I would have liked to stop and take a break, but we weren't allowed any unauthorized time. The machines were very big and very difficult to operate, but in time I got used to the size and the noise.

But I never quite got used to the accidents some of the women had because they weren't paying attention or somehow they judged wrong. There were several women who lost their fingers, hands or even their arms, depending on the machine they had been working on.

There were days when I could barely keep my eyes open or listen to the clambering of the machines. That was because on those days, after being up almost all night entertaining the Gestapo, I was so tired I wanted to just take off and never come back.

There were also those occasions when my imagination would take over and I would hear the songs my mother used to sing to us. The words echoed back and forth in my ears, and sometimes I would start to cry. I would then try my best not to have Dora see me, but Dora always watched. Even when I didn't see her watching me, I knew she was.

I didn't seem to adjust as well as I should have when we worked, but that was probably because I was a lot younger than most of the other women. Certainly having Dora's help got me through some of the rougher days, and there were plenty of those.

Late at night, when no one seemed to be watching and I couldn't sleep, Dora and I would have conversations. Dora always encouraged my dreams and sometimes we would talk about what we would do when we were free. Maybe we'd go directly to Hollywood, where I could start my career. It never mattered where we were going, only that we were going to go somewhere.

We planned a new life, even if we were never going to have one. You can't give up your dreams just like that. Hope is what took us from one day to the next.

What Does it Take to Survive?

What does it take to survive? I'm not sure that I'll ever know the answer to that.

As the hours passed into days and the days into months, I tried to accept the horrible way in which we lived. Sometimes I almost forgot what it was like to be able to have a choice. Even a simple function like going to the bathroom was supervised.

For the most part, we did as we were told. However, there were the rebels, with a mind of their own and lots of courage. Women like Irene.

Irene had beautiful blonde hair and green eyes. She hated following orders, but somehow she always managed to give in right before things got serious. She liked to toy with the Gestapo guards, trying to see just how far she could push.

There was one day when she pushed too far and even she couldn't help herself. It was at the end of the day, when we were just about to start the long march back to our barracks. Irene had just asked for permission to have a bathroom break. She took longer than usual, and one of the Gestapo women went in to get her. As the rest of us stood there waiting, we heard a voice yell out from the bathroom, "Damn you. Get that cigarette out of your mouth now!"

We stood in line, unresponsive, waiting for departure instructions. But instead of our instructions, one of the Gestapo came over to me and shouted, "Go and get your friend out of there."

As always, I obeyed the Gestapo. Slowly, I walked into the bathroom, not knowing what to expect. I was shocked when I took a look at Irene. She was standing against the bathroom wall, smoking a cigarette.

"Have you gone mad? You had better get that cigarette out of your mouth right now and come with me," I said as I reached for her hand.

Irene's eyes were filled with anger. "Who the hell do they think they are, telling me what to do? If I want to smoke, I'll smoke."

I responded to Irene's questions quickly. "They are Hitler's women," I said. "We have to do as they say."

Irene's response was angered. "You might have to, but not me. Not anymore."

It happened so fast I barely had time to close my eyes. The Gestapo soldier nudged me and said, "Open up your eyes. Everyone watches."

There were three Gestapo soldiers who dragged Irene out right in the center of the workshop. We were all told to stand right behind them. Then, with swiftness and skill, the soldiers took turns kicking and poking Irene with a gun.

The largest of the three Gestapo women stood before Irene and shouted, "Sit on your knees and beg us to stop Jew. Now! Do it Jew. Now!"

By this time, Irene could no longer speak.

The three Gestapo women laughed in her face, " Too bad Juden. Too bad."

It was fast. One of the women leaned down while holding a scissors in one hand and started to cut Irene's hair off. In a matter of minutes, Irene's beautiful blond hair was lying on the ground. Irene was completely bald and unconscious.

Seconds later, one of the other Gestapo women pointed to me and two other women. "Now that you've seen the show, get rid of her. Bring her outside."

We did as they asked and then, without a word, we marched back to our barracks without Irene. That night none of us slept. When Irene was not brought back in the morning, we knew she was dead.

Letter To Me –

For days I couldn't get the vision of Irene leaning against the bathroom wall smoking what turned out to be her last cigarette out of my mind. She was so beautiful but so angry. I was angry but I wanted to live. I don't think she did. Sometimes when everyone else is sleeping and it's very, very quiet, I sit up and look around at all these very wonderful women who have so much to give and wonder if they will ever get out of here. Then I wonder if I'll ever get out of here. Then I look around again and I 'm not quite sure any of us will ever get out of here alive.

—Me

Everyone Loved Dora

Everyone loved Dora. She was admired by all the women in our barracks, not only for her kindness but because she was a good leader. She was everyone's mother and everyone's friend. She never complained when the going got tough. And tough it was.

Early on, Dora discovered to reach that pot of gold at the end of the rainbow, she would have to do whatever the Gestapo asked. If it meant cleaning that extra pot or doing that one last chore, she did it with good reason. Her reward was food, and without the least bit of selfishness, she shared whatever she was given. Usually the one with the most threatening circumstances was given the extra food, sometimes it was me. I was very skinny, as were most of the others.

The Gestapo had a one-track mind – how much could we produce? And if we didn't produce, we would be transported to a death camp. It was very uncomfortable living with that black cloud of smoke hanging over you.

But it was Dora who kept our morale up. I was certain she was my guardian angel. Dora would have done anything for me, fight any battle, whatever it took. She was there for me, even if it jeopardized her own safety. In everything she did and in everything she said, I was very happy to have her in my corner.

Oddly enough, the days passed quickly with very little time to think of everything we knew and every dream we had. However, we did know when the most blessed day of the Jewish year, Yom Kippur, had arrived. Dora asked for permission for us to have a small service after work. At first the Gestapo said no, but then on the eve of Yom Kippur, permission was granted. I often wondered how many extra pots or toilets Dora had to scrub for that one night of prayer.

That evening, we came back to our barracks very tired. The Gestapo worked us extra hard that day. Certainly, they weren't about to give us one night of prayer without an extra pile of work. Compassion was not a strong suit for the Gestapo.

It was after sundown when Dora began the service. It was as if G-d was with us. Dora, in perfect tone, led us as we started to pray. There was not a dry eye among us, each remembering our loved ones. We held hands as we wept. My heart was broken.

Moments before Dora was about to close the service, she looked at me and smiled. Right at that very moment, I believed we would someday be free. G-d would help us. I knew G-d was in that room crying with us.

Before finishing the service, Dora stood completely still and looked around the room. A pin could have dropped and you would have heard it.

Dora finished with, "Hear oh Israel, the Lord our G-d, the Lord is one. Blessed be the name of His glorious kingdom forever and ever. Have mercy upon us and destroy us not. Be with us yet to the end, our comforter of tomorrow. Amen."

As the weather changed and the cold air filtered in, several of the women in our barracks became sick. We tried to cover for them as much as possible, because anybody sick went straight to the crematoriums we had all heard so much about. Sick Jews were worthless, that's what they'd say, and we believed them.

Dora and I would give our food to anyone sick so they could regain their strength. Sometimes it worked, but then there were the times when someone was just too sick to pretend.

That was Ina. She slept in the bed next to mine. For more than a week she coughed into her sleeve, trying to muffle the sound from her raspy throat. Every day, she became weaker than the day before. On several occasions, Dora got her an extra bowl of soup, but she was even too weak to sip the soup.

Dora whispered to Ina, "Please try to get the soup down. You need to get your strength back. Please do it for me."

But she couldn't. That night Ina couldn't stop coughing. Her face was flushed and her eyes were glassy. I motioned to Ina, trying to get her attention. I wanted to tell her to put her blanket over her face when she coughed, but she didn't see me. She was in bad shape.

Dora stood up and pretended to be going to the bathroom. Dora whispered to Ina, "Please lay down and cough into your pillow. They'll hear you."

When she didn't lie down, I knew that night might be Ina's last with us. It was. In the morning when I got up, Ina wasn't there. She never returned.

Is This the End?

As the Germans started to lose the war, the work camps were being phased out. We weren't told much, but every so often the gossip seemed to be breezing through the air. The threat of being gassed in the big chambers was what everyone talked about.

I think Dora knew a lot more than she discussed. She wanted to protect me from everything, but that was impossible. I listened to the others and I prayed what they said wasn't true.

They said the Gestapo was going to march us to a concentration camp, gas us and then dispose of us in the usual manner, which meant being buried or burned. Both were scary. That was how we lived, waiting to die.

At our work camp there were approximately nine hundred women. We were divided into three groups, and each group was to have one woman in charge. The Transport Fuhrer was the name given to the holder of that position. Dora was our Transport Fuhrer.

Not just any woman was given that job. The woman chosen for that position had to be extremely trustworthy and capable, certainly reasons why Dora was chosen. The Gestapo had known Dora longer than most of the others, and she had always followed orders just as the Germans had given them. When Dora promised her extreme loyalty, the Gestapo believed her. She was honest as the day was long.

The day we left was bitter cold. We didn't have warm coats or boots to keep us warm, but still we were ordered to march, and march was exactly what we did. We marched highway to highway, farmland to farmland.

At this point in our journey, we were no longer getting orders from Gestapo women. The Gestapo men were now giving us instructions. They were extremely physically able and unfortunately, we were not. We were weakened and they knew it, but still they marched us hard. Somewhere between ready to collapse and physically unable, they stopped us.

Immediately after stopping, Dora walked toward the front of the line and spoke up to one of the Gestapo soldiers. "Please, my girls are frozen," she said. "Look at their feet. Please I beg of you, take them out of their misery."

The Gestapo soldier looked at Dora with a grin on his face and said, "I will decide when and where to stop and who lives or dies or gets shot or doesn't. So get the girls ready and we will begin."

Dora waved us on and once again we began to march. There were no set provisions for us. Whether or not we ate never seemed to be anyone's utmost concern. We definitely would have been able to march a lot faster had we been given some nourishment, but no one ever said the Gestapo was smart.

It was unbearably cold during our march, but at sundown we did get to stop. Dora, in her usual straightforward approach, politely looked up at one of the Gestapo guards. "Please let my girls go across the field and into the farms for some food. Maybe the farmers will feel generous."

"And maybe they won't," the guard shouted.

Dora continued to pursue the issue. "Please let them try."

"And what if they don't come back?" insisted the officer.

With sincerity in her eyes, Dora responded, "My girls won't disappoint me."

The Gestapo officer proceeded to pull me toward him. He held a gun to my head as he spoke to Dora. "They can go, but not all at once. If they don't return, and I mean if even one of them doesn't come back, your sister will die."

Dora nodded in agreement and the guard released me. My heart was beating double time as I flew into Dora's arms for comfort. I stayed with Dora until every last one of the girls came back.

Later that night when we were alone, I whispered to Dora, "Please let's escape. We don't look Jewish, that's what everyone says. We can do it."

With a great sense of commitment and courage, Dora whispered back, "Salucia my child, whatever happens to my girls must happen to me too. We stay." I admired my sister's loyalty and I really found it commendable, but on the other hand I still wanted to escape. We didn't, but we should have.

Regardless of how tired or cold we were, the Gestapo had us walking. We walked through Prague and Czechoslovakia, with very little stopping time or sometimes none. Beside the freezing cold environment, we were put to the test on a daily basis.

Everywhere we walked, Hitler's children greeted us. In every new location, city or village we passed through, we were treated with the same form of humiliation from Hitler's children. The children would shout out in a chanting fashion, "Die Juden, die!"

And if that wasn't enough, everywhere we walked the children threw rocks at us. They probably had no idea why they hated us.

When we arrived at Resinger Flossenberg Concentration Camp, we were exhausted. After all, we had marched close to six hundred horrible miles. We had hoped that the Gestapo would let us sleep, even if only for a short time, but we were wrong.

They brought us into a large room and ordered us to undress. Before we undressed, it was explained to us that we would be able to retrieve whatever we had placed in the pile after our shower. Dora and I looked at each other for what appeared to be one of the last times. It was true. The gossip, the showers, it was all true.

I tearfully watched as the other women placed their belongings in the pile.

Some had folded pictures they had carried with them for years. They each took one last, wonderful look at their families and friends smiling at them in the photos. I had nothing to throw in the pile except what I had been wearing. I didn't know if that was good or bad, but to me it seemed very sad.

Moments later, one of the Gestapo officers shouted to us again, "Take off your clothes now!"

We did as we were told. Modesty was of little importance. We were ordered to walk single file into another room. Why didn't they just shoot us? It would have been faster.

Suddenly, a commotion broke out in back of the line. One of the women screamed out in a panic, "Please don't do this. Please!"

Enraged, one of the Gestapo officers pulled out his gun and placed it right in the middle of the woman's forehead. "Follow me," he shouted.

Shivering from the cold, we continued walking. When a gunshot bellowed through the air, we knew the woman who begged on our behalf was killed.

It seemed as if we had been walking for hours, when it really had only been minutes. We then entered a huge bathroom, which adjoined an even larger room, certainly not big enough for the nearly three hundred women who were crowded inside.

Dora inched her way up to be closer to me, and then took my hand and squeezed it tightly. "It's going to be OK," she whispered.

By this time my eyes had filled up with tears. "No it's not, but thank you for loving me enough to say so."

Dora kissed my forehead and we stood there, ready for whatever came next.

With a loud noise coming from the pipes, the water was turned on. The water continued to come down at various intervals until it was replaced with a cloud of smoke. By this time, my hand was raw from the tightness of Dora's hold. Then with one quick motion, the water was shut off. Dora and I looked at each other.

Dora shouted with delight, "Oh my G-d we're alive. We didn't die."

I pinched my skin. Dora was right. We were alive. Still nude, we stood there shivering but happy, waiting for instructions.

When the Gestapo handed out striped dresses, we knew whatever belongings we had were gone forever. Shameful as it was, the Gestapo soldiers took whatever they wanted and burned the rest. They were trying to erase the memories of our heritage. What the Gestapo didn't know was our memories would remain in our hearts for years to come, some privately, some publicly. But they could never take that from us. Never.

Human nature has a way of releasing tension. As the dresses were passed out, they weren't sized. In a somewhat chaotic situation, we found ourselves laughing as each of us tried to find the right size. Some dresses were down to the floor, while others barely covered the thighs. And when the wooden shoes were passed out, we were really a sight. When we laughed, I thought I had forgotten how.

It wasn't long after the laughter began when we heard the click of the Gestapo boots coming toward us. A Gestapo guard marched in shouting, "Everyone stay right where you are. Don't move."

Several other Gestapo guards entered carrying long sticks. We all stood in fear of what was yet to come. Had we been spared, or was the end near? None of us knew.

Dora looked my way. She shrugged her shoulders, unsure of what was about to happen. There hadn't been any gossip about this.

Just when you think being dehumanized has taken its height, something even more horrible than you can imagine occurs. The Gestapo started to mark the heads of all the women with what looked like a branding iron for cattle. I had never received a number on my arm, so I assumed that was what came next. I was wrong. They were numbering us in groups – one, one and a half, two, two and a half, and three. Dora and I were both numbered one. What that meant we did not know.

When the branding was finished, we were moved into another room. I had hoped for a sip of soup or a nibble of bread, but we were not fed, nor were we going to be.

With a thunderous scream one of the Gestapo shouted, "It's time to go. Line up. Juden, line up. Now!"

As we had done so many times before, we lined up like soldiers waiting to fight yet another battle. Then, from behind the line, one of the Gestapo soldiers shoved into me. When he walked away, I noticed he had shoved a sandwich under my arm. I was too scared to move, so I left it right where it was and continued to march with the others.

As we marched, I kept wondering why he had given me the sandwich. I found it hard to believe that any Gestapo soldier could care about any of us, if only for a moment. I may have been wrong. I had met one who had.

Several days later, even as the weather became colder and colder, we still marched. Our instructions were to stay close to each other, especially as we marched up the very steep hills that would take us to our next stopover. When we arrived at the barn, once again we had been denied food or water.

Later that night, when the Gestapo had too much to drink and had passed out, I held up my sandwich and called out to the women in our barracks who were still up, "Look at what I have for us."

It was only a cheese sandwich, but for us it was gourmet. Each woman took a small bite. It wasn't nourishing, but it was good. After that, most of us fell right to sleep from sheer exhaustion.

In the morning when we awoke, I looked around at these loving women who seemingly cared about each other and I knew we were blessed by a guardian angel who was traveling with us.

Letter To Me –

One might wonder, as I did, how we managed to stay alive. We don't have warm coats or boots, not even gloves to keep our hands warm. So how, in the middle of winter, are we staying alive without food and with only the drippings from the toilet to keep us hydrated? Please dear G-d, if we don't have angels at our side, how do we live yet another day?

—Me

Give Me Strength

When we talk of strength and bravery, we rarely talk about ourselves. But why not? We came through the darkest tunnel at the most inopportune time, winter.

Sometimes when those sharp winds blew in our faces, we could barely breathe. It was unbearable at best, but still we marched and we slept and then we marched some more. We had hoped that the weather would ease up but it didn't, in fact it grew worse. We didn't complain, because who would listen? There were several women who did whatever they could to get themselves inside and out of the cold, like Anna.

Dora and I were in line with a woman about Dora's age, in her early twenties. She called herself Anna, and even in the most trying of situations tried to keep her spunky personality in check. It was colder than usual that day. "I'm going to pretend to faint," she whispered. "When I fall back into your arms, hold me."

Dora and I nodded back to her.

It didn't take but a minute until Anna leaned back into Dora and my arms. "Oh my ... whee," she called out right before she fell into our arms.

Immediately the Gestapo guard walked over to us and shouted, "Get her inside. Now!"

As we carried Anna inside, she gave us a wink. At least for that day we got to stay inside and be warm, but on the next day we were right back outside in the freezing cold.

It had been days since we were branded with numbers on our forehead and we still had no idea why. Then one day while we were outside, a rock came from across the fence. Dora picked up the rock and opened the piece of paper that had been attached to it. After reading the paper, she looked across at the young man who had thrown it. He then ran off.

Dora didn't want to tell anyone what the note read, but several of us who noticed her face turning white wanted to know.

"Dora, please you have to tell us. What is it? Please Dora," I repeated. Instead of answering our questions, Dora took her hand and tried to rub the number one from my forehead.

Dora was rubbing so hard it hurt. "What are you doing?" I asked, trying to pull her hand from my forehead. "It hurts."

Dora looked into my eyes. "I can't let them touch you. These numbers are for the Gestapo soldiers. Each of us is to be divided into groups. We're their play toys, for sex. They want us for sex. But they won't touch you. You're too young. I won't let them. They'll have to kill me first."

It was then that a whistle was heard coming down the track. It was the train for us, but it was several days early. There was so much commotion when the trains pulled in the Gestapo had very little time to get us ready. They had no patience with anyone who questioned them. Those who did were either beaten or shot, their usual way of handling us.

Dora stood beside me. She grabbed my hand and held on tightly. "Don't let go for even a minute," Dora said. "We're not going to be separated. We can't be." While we waited, Dora and I noticed the young man who threw the rock watching us. Dora nodded, thanking him for his warning, and he nodded back.

From the moment we boarded the trains we were treated like cattle. Actually, cattle would have been better off than we were. We were shoved into the dark cars and, after a while, we had no idea if it were morning, afternoon or night. We were given no food or water, which made us wonder what we were being punished for.

It was all so hateful, especially when the Gestapo threw us into the cars and locked us in. At first we talked among ourselves, but after a while we barely spoke. There were times when I had to fight for a breath of air. Even if we wanted to escape, it would have been impossible. There was no running. Either we lived or we died, and at that point no one would have cared either way.

There were so many questions, but the one I most would have liked to answer is how they could be so cruel as to treat human beings in such a distasteful way, locking us in without bathroom facilities. There were times when I thought if I didn't get off the train I would scream, but I didn't. I just sat there like the others, wondering if after this humiliating, dehumanizing experience, if I would be alive. Or more importantly, would I even want to be?

As the train rolled on, we heard bombing, and sometimes out of sheer desperation, I wished a bomb would hit the train and it would all be over. I kept my thoughts to myself, one reason being I had no idea who was next to me.

It was because of the extreme darkness that my eyes weakened, as I'm certain everyone else's did. We were all in our own private hell, and what each of us did to stay alive was private.

My escape was hearing my mother's sweet voice singing to me. Her voice was so beautiful and loving, just the mere thought of the words she sang to us made everything seem easier.

Sometimes when I closed my eyes very tight, I could hear my mother's voice whispering to me, "Salucia, my child, just hold on a little while longer. Dora is with you, and you will see G-d will give you strength."

When the trains stopped and the doors unlocked, we were blinded by the daylight. It wasn't long before the Gestapo shoved us out of the cars and into an open field. At first I didn't see Dora, but after my eyes became accustomed to daylight, I found her. She was covered from head to toe with dirt from the coal car. We hugged each other tightly for the longest time.

One of the first things the Gestapo soldiers had us do was go back into the coal cars and remove the dead bodies. Once more, we had to accustom our eyes to the darkness of the train. Reentering the cars was quite difficult. The smell was so horrible. The only way you could walk through the cars was by holding your breath for short periods of time.

After all of the dead bodies were removed and buried, we were told to line up. By this time we were all so exhausted and hungry we couldn't see straight, but the Gestapo had plans for us. We were to start marching and not stop until they told us to. I wasn't the only one with tears of exhaustion in my eyes, but when they said, "March," we marched.

When we approached our destination, the words rang out to me as I looked at the sign over the gate, "HERE YOU ARE TO BE FINISHED ... Finiceted dune." We were now at Bergen Belson. This was the end of the road for us. As I looked around at the mere skeletons of women before me, I didn't know if I was relieved or upset.

Dora whispered in my ear, "Are you going to be OK?"

"Yes, I m going to be just fine," I answered with slight regret. "We should have escaped when we had the chance. Now that we're here, it's a little too late to question why."

"I'm so sorry," Dora said as she reached for my hand and held it tighter than ever before. "I still have hope. What about you?"

"I don't know. Maybe a little, but I wish you didn't have to be a mother to the whole world."

"My girls need me," Dora answered.

I tried to understand why Dora felt the need to be there for all her girls, but selfishly I really wished we could have escaped. But the other side of me watched the girls as they looked at Dora when she spoke to them. They had so much love and appreciation for her kindness and sensibility. She brought sunshine to them and they loved her for it, and so did I.

When the Gestapo finally decided we had marched long enough, the soldiers ordered us to stop. We were then taken to a very large barracks, where many other women lay on the ground looking sadly uncomfortable. The floors were concrete and it was very cold inside. Everywhere you walked there were other Jews layered over each other. The sleeping space was so tight you could hardly breath and as you walked, you had to be very careful you didn't step on someone's head. The very moment I found a spot, without a blanket or anything to give me comfort, I fell right asleep.

By this time I began to lose track of time. We were too weak to fight and too angry to cry, and the days and nights didn't seem very different. We had learned to function with very little nourishment, although every now and then the Gestapo brought us a large kettle of soup to be divided by hundreds. Sometimes it was better not to eat at all than to be teased into a meal consisting of several sips of soups and scraps of bread, not enough for even a mouse.

There was one day in particular that comes to mind. The soup kettle had been brought in by one of the larger woman and placed on the floor. It was so hot the steam filtered the air, making it smell almost good. Several of the women pushed their way right to the front of the line, causing some of the other women to savagely push back.

Then, with the flash of the eye, the entire kettle fell over and the hot soup was everywhere. It was horrifying to see so many of the women kneeling on the ground, trying to scoop up what they could of the potato soup.

All of a sudden, three of the Gestapo guards shouted simultaneously. "Who did this? Come clean this up now!"

When no one answered, the guards were even angrier. Some of the women didn't know my name nor I theirs, but we were a family. If we didn't have each other, then who did we have?

Because of that one instance, we weren't given any food for days and the only available liquid, as always, was the toilet water from outside. I couldn't help but wonder. How much is enough? Didn't they see what we were going through? How could humans treat each other this way? According to the Gestapo, we deserved to die. How could that be, and why should it be? There were so many questions but there were no answers. I wanted to believe this horror would stop, but it was getting to the point where I had begun to think this horror would never end.

The days passed quickly, but the nights were never-ending. I woke up inhaling and exhaling the smoke of the burning bodies coming from the crematoriums. There were dead bodies everywhere.

Then there was the problem of the escalating war. The Germans didn't want the American or British soldiers to find out just how many Jewish people were killed, so as fast as the Germans killed them, they disposed of them. The murders never seemed to stop, and neither did the burning of bodies. Men, women and children would no longer be families.

In Sickness and in Health

One of the major problems for us in the camps was typhus. The only problem was if we got too weak, we were taken away. If anyone got typhus, they tried their best to act as if they were well. This was extremely hard, almost impossible.

Dora became one of the victims of typhus. She had such horrible stomach pains she could barely stand, but if anyone could possibly pretend to be healthy, it was Dora. Certainly, one reason she couldn't tell anyone she was sick was because of me. If we were separated, even for a day, we might never find each other again. Neither one of us wanted that, so I did what I could to help her, we all did. Just to play it safe, if Dora needed help walking, several of the women walked behind her, making sure she didn't fall over.

Then there was that day when you look up at the sky and you think you see G-d, and then for a moment everything stops. You wonder how this horrible mess started and if it will ever end. You know you just can't take any more of this misery and heartache and you feel if you screamed for an hour, it wouldn't be enough.

You then stop looking up and you close your eyes for just a second or two, hoping that your prayers will be answered. Then it happens, and everything changes. Life becomes good and you get that sign from above that there really is a G-d.

That's exactly what happened. Just as everything seemed hopeless and the Gestapo was never going to stop the murdering, it stopped. Finally it was over.

Right in the middle of the day, the Gestapo soldiers packed up their things and left. They never said goodbye and neither did we. Those horrible men and women with guns and knives and terrible voices were gone.

Dora, who had been so very ill, smiled at me and asked, "Do you hear the music?"

"Music?" I questioned. "You hear music?" I was certain Dora's fever had gone way above the normal limits.

Again I listened. Then, with a faint distant tone, I also heard the music. I gave Dora a great big hug. "It's going to be OK."

A short time later, the music became louder, and as we looked outside the barracks we saw the British troops coming to get us. They were the knights in shinning armor. They were messengers from heaven. G-d heard me pray and he answered.

Freedom

There was music and dancing in the streets. We danced, even those of us who didn't feel well. We were celebrating with G-d. We were being allowed to come back into the world. We were free. We could inhale and exhale without a gun to our back, certainly reason enough to rejoice. This was a day I would never forget. I had my life back. I was ready to make all my dreams become reality. I was ready to celebrate the greatest gift of all, life. However, first I would have to get my strength back.

Conditions were chaotic. Men, women and children were being transported to barracks that were safe from the rampant typhus. Food was being distributed to all of us, but because we had been deprived of food for such a very long time, our stomachs couldn't handle the intrusion of food. Those who tried to eat often overate and became quite sick. Some died.

Once again, Dora was there to protect me and make sure everything went all right. When Dora realized how sick I really was, she whispered to me, "Whatever you do, don't tell anyone you're sick, and most importantly, smile."

As always, Dora was right. Later that day, we were approached to seek medical help, but each time an American or British soldier came near us, Dora looked at them and answered, "We're fine, and thank you for asking." Her tone was abrupt, but after that, no one bothered us.

As soon as the soldiers were far from sight, Dora patted my back in her usual reassuring way and said, "You did fine. We've come too far to be separated now. After all of this, we couldn't lose each other. Not now, not ever."

Dora was absolutely right. After all we'd gone through, I wasn't about to lose her. The thought of life without her seemed impossible.

The days that followed were vague. It was very hard to get back into the real world and I assumed everyone else felt that way too. We had been prisoners in our own bodies for so long that becoming normal, so to speak, was quite difficult. Even going to the bathroom and taking showers were blessed events. The simple tasks and pleasures of life were taken away from us for so long that even being allowed to have a drink of water, whenever or wherever you wanted, seemed like a luxury.

I can only speak for myself, but it was very difficult to adjust to freedom. On the other hand, it was quite wonderful. It was a time of confusion for all of us, but we were thankful for this time.

Many of the other survivors roamed the streets searching for loved ones. They were looking for a familiar face, anything to help make them feel as if they belonged. We were all strangers, even to ourselves. I was one of the lucky ones. I had Dora.

For days, Dora and I asked everyone we saw if anyone knew our brothers or if they had any idea where they could be. Just as we had come to accept the fact that we may never locate Phillip and David, word of the Red Cross registering families became known to us.

Immediatley, Dora and I went to register. There were so many people waiting in line, each as hopeful as Dora and I were. The Red Cross volunteers were wonderfully helpful. They helped those who were too weak to walk and fed those who needed to regain their strength.

The volunteers gave us the attention we needed, even if it meant holding our hands or reassuring us that in time everything would be fine. That was an easy thought to hang on to. In fact, it was with those thoughts I was able to carry on. Holding on was what this whole horrible ordeal was about. After all, hadn't I already proved that?

After being transported to Gosla, a small town in Germany, we were put up in hotels. These hotels were being used solely for our purposes. It felt so right, so human. For such a very long time we were treated as if we were animals, but Dora and I were really looking forward to mainstreaming back into life.

Shortly after we arrived in Gosla, Dora and I registered with the Red Cross office, just in case there was any news about Philip and David. We were then fed, clothed and able to take showers. Life could begin again. Even Dora became much more relaxed and we were both trying to regain trust, which we knew would take much longer.

I noticed Dora had seemed very different. She seemed happy. I had no idea what had turned her around so fast, until I noticed her talking to a young man seated in the hotel lobby. She was smiling and seemingly very comfortable in her conversation with him.

When she saw me watching, she motioned for me to join her. I had no idea just how important this young man would be in both of our lives.

Dora smiled as she introduced us, "Sala, meet Irving. Irving, meet Sala."

Immediatley, I could sense they liked each other, a perfect match. And I was right. From that day forward, Dora and Irving were a twosome, and that was fine with me. Just as I knew Dora had found her soul mate, I knew it was going to be a very long time before I did. Being in love was not in my plan.

I had a career to think about and arrange. Sometimes I wondered why I wanted so much more than anyone else. In the camps my thoughts were consumed by my desire to be famous. I wanted to sing and dance as I'd never done before. I wanted to be famous, someone people would remember. I was going to go to America, land of opportunity and great fortune. I was going to be a star and I wasn't about to let anyone interfere with my plans or to tell me different.

It didn't take long for me to realize it wasn't going to be as easy as I had hoped. Just because we had been liberated from the Nazi camps and Hitler's Gestapo didn't mean that people instantly accepted Jewish men, women and children in their communities. There was still that undertone that existed. Just because we wanted to end the hatred didn't mean the world was quite ready to oblige us.

When Will It Be Over?

It was a sunny day. We had just begun to feel as if life could once again be beautiful and painless. Dora, several other young men and women and I were once again tempted by the delights of freedom and the joys of laughter. We were all seated at a round table in an ice cream parlor near our hotel when, once again, that cloud of black smoke appeared in front of us.

We were talking among ourselves, not paying much attention to anything else. I happened to glance outside to the British soldiers who were on watch, not thinking about why they were there, when a sudden loud voice bellowed out.

"It's not true about the concentration camps. The Jews lie. They should all die. Who needs Jews in this world? They should all get out!"

Without knowing how to respond, I watched as one of the young men at our table stood up and shouted back to the man who was so uncivilized. "Are you telling me there were no murders? If you're telling me this, then you tell me – where are my parents ... my grandparents and my baby sister?"

Then another young man stood up and shouted, "And my brothers, where are they? You bastard."

The German man laughed, "Who cares?"

Once again, the first young man who spoke yelled in anger, "Tell me why my family does not sit here with me. If you say nothing happened, then you tell me – where are all those I loved?"

The German seated at the table behind us laughed, "Who cares? Anyway, the only good Jew is a dead one."

Angered by the German's words, the young man who was with us took a swing at the German and then, without a thought, everyone from our table stood, as did the others from the table behind us.

One punch led to another, and what started as one punch snowballed into quite a fistfight. Soon, everyone started pushing and shoving – utter confusion had begun. Tables went flying; dishes and silverware were thrown in the air. In a matter of moments, the British soldiers from outside were now inside, pulling us apart. So it began. The healing was going to take a long time.

Like clockwork, every few days Dora and I went to the Red Cross office, hoping that there would be good news for us about our brothers, but as usual we left disappointed. They told us we didn't have to come as frequently, so we nodded in agreement. But in a few days when they told us the same thing, we knew in a few more days we would be back again. Dora and I were very persistent. We never discussed the possibility of our brothers not being alive. Somewhere in our hearts, we knew Philip and David were alive. We weren't being foolish. Some things you just know.

Dora and I kept hoping to hear news about our brothers, but there was none. We decided to go on with our lives while we waited for the Red Cross to locate them. We imagined somewhere out there, they were just as anxious to find us. I had faith in the knowledge that we would soon find each other.

While we waited for the news about our brothers, Dora and Irving decided to get married. They certainly had my blessing. Irving was such a kind, loving man. He definitely had my vote.

Because Dora was such a wonderful sister and Irving was the kindest brother-in-law one could have, they asked me to live with them. At first I said no, but they insisted, so I did. Together, we started to build our lives. Dora and Irving were very happy with each other, but I still had my dreams.

I refused to believe my talents began and ended entertaining the Gestapo. I didn't tell anyone about my innermost thoughts, even Dora. She wouldn't want me to be disappointed. How could I tell her how incomplete I felt? After all, I had survived what six million did not. I must be selfish.

Then the unthinkable happened. I had just entered the apartment when Dora motioned for me to have a seat on the sofa. She sat next to me.

"I want you to meet someone," she said as she gave my hand a squeeze.

"Meet who?" I asked, confused by her offer.

"A nice young man. He's a friend of Irving's. His name is Ben."

Dora had completely caught me off guard. I wasn't looking for a man. I had far too much to accomplish before I gave my heart to any man.

"Dora, you know I have no time for a man right now."

Dora smiled at me, "I just want to see you as happy as I am."

"And I will be, but not right now. I have my dreams."

By this time, I didn't know what to say. On one hand, I just wanted to walk out of the apartment and forget about the conversation we had just had, but I knew Dora wouldn't let me. I could see it in her eyes. She was serious.

"Dora, I have so many things I want to do. You know my dreams."

"It's just a date. A dinner. That's all," Dora added. "What harm can it do? Please, just do it for me."

"Maybe some other time," I said as I stood up, ready to leave the room.

Dora hesitated for a moment, "But I promised Ben."

I felt my face redden as I cried out, "Dora how could you do this to me?"

"I'm doing this because I love you." Dora was appealing to my guilt. "I just want you to be happy."

I should have never gone but I did. The evening went fairly well, but there wasn't a moment of that night when I didn't wish I wasn't there.

Just as Dora had insisted, she had fixed me up with Ben because she loved me, was the very reason I decided to marry Ben. I did it for Dora, certainly not for me. Several weeks later, Ben and I were married. We lived as man and wife. But somehow I never felt married. Ben worked long hours while I stayed home, cooked, cleaned and dreamt of what my life would have been like had I never married. My life was definitely much different than I had imagined. Dora and Irving seemed convinced that in time I would accept my life as typical, possibly one of the reasons I was so unhappy. Ordinary wasn't what I wanted.

But soon I grew into my life. I was determined to try making myself happy, even if I knew it would be difficult.

A Day to Remember

Life has a way of working out doubts and uncertainties. In this case, the much-awaited news of Phillip and David's arrival put everything in its proper perspective. Dora and I were both very excited about our good news — everything else we did came in a close second. Every other word out of our mouths was about our brothers, and rightfully so. We were going to be a family again. Life does go on.

Finally, the day arrived. Dora, Irving, Ben and I were all there, waving them on. My knees were weak and my stomach had butterflies. I wondered if we would all still feel the same as we did before the war. As the train pulled in and all the passengers came, I saw the two of them, and it was as if time hadn't passed at all. My brothers were as handsome as ever.

We hugged each other so tightly we could barely breathe. It was a feeling like no other. Without saying it, I knew Dora was as happy as I was. I could sense it even through the tears. After several hugs and kisses, I realized they each had a woman beside them.

Phillip did the introductions. "This is my fiancee, Sophie. You remember her. She lived down the street from us. And Erica, David's wife, she too was from the old neighborhood."

As I listened to Phillip I couldn't help but think how thrilled my parents would have been to meet the new additions to our family. Our family was growing, and that was very good. Dora and I spent as much time with them as possible, trying to find them suitable housing. In a matter of weeks, my brothers were well on their way toward starting a new life.

For a Change, Something is Right

I ran all the way to Dora's apartment with a smile on face. I could not wait to tell her the news. I remember knocking on the door so hard my knuckles were red. When Dora opened the door, I ran into her arms.

"So are you?" she asked.

I was still out of breath from running, but when I nodded, I didn't have to say another word. She knew. Dora took my hand and sat me down at the kitchen table.

Dora called out, "Irving come quick. Hurry."

Irving came running into the kitchen, "What's wrong?"

Dora motioned for Irving to sit down before she answered, "For a change, something is right."

Dora looked at me to get my approval to tell Irving. I could tell she was so excited, if she didn't tell him right at that very moment, she would burst.

"Be my guest. Tell him."

"Tell me what?" Irving said. "Tell me what?"

"We're pregnant. Sala's going to have a baby." Dora then looked up and said, "You see. G-d is good, very good."

If nothing ever happened in my life again, just watching Dora enjoy my pregnancy made everything worthwhile. To see her eyes light up in such joy made me realize just how special she really was. She was a sister like no other. She was just as much a part of me as I was of her.

I had been so busy in my own thoughts that I hadn't even noticed Dora bringing out the wine and glasses. With a very endearing smile, Irving raised his glass. "To life. L'chaim."

For a moment or two, I watched these two very special people salute my child to be and I. Inside my heart, I knew I had done something so wonderful, a mitzvah, for Dora and Irving. They were so much more to me than a brother-in-law and sister. They were like my parents; they were perfect.

The next six months flew by. There were days when I did nothing but lie in bed, thinking about my new baby and how very lucky I was to be getting a chance to be someone's mother. I couldn't say marriage had any bearing on my happiness, because it didn't.

When I thought of my baby, Ben wasn't even in the picture. In fact, for those six months I barely saw him, which on most days didn't bother me in the least. But then there were the days of loneliness and the thoughts of sharing a life with a man I loved that haunted my nights. Ben was not that man, and I wondered if there would ever be that one special man.

Ben was usually late for dinner, but when he finally did get home I never asked why. It didn't seem to matter, and the less said the better. But there was that one night. I guess I was feeling sorry for myself. It was after seven when I decided that if he couldn't come home on time, I wasn't going to wait. If he didn't like it, it was too damn bad.

I sat at the table, slowly sipping some water. I didn't even turn around when the door opened and he walked in. Ben wasn't very quiet when he was out with others, but with me he had very little to say.

As he washed his hands, preparing to sit down, I don't know what came over me. I looked at him and asked, "And where were you?"

As he sat down he answered rather abruptly, "At work, why?"

"Every night?"

He seemed shocked by my response, so I decided to let it ride. I didn't want to make a big deal about something I usually didn't care about. But as I looked into his eyes, I knew the conversation was about to take a turn for the worse.

Ben looked me square in the eye and said, "I didn't think you cared."

"I don't. I'm just sick and tired of sitting here night after night, eating dinner alone. Why bother to come home at all?"

Getting angrier, Ben's voice raised to a much higher level. "I didn't think it was because you missed me."

I wished I could have told him I missed him, and then he would have taken me in his arms and told me everything was going to be fine. I wanted it to be like it was in the movies, where everyone lived happily ever after. It didn't happen that way at all. In fact, that night neither of us said another word to each other.

We finished dinner in silence and when it was time to go to bed, we never even said goodnight. I remembered thinking it was such a shame. It was obvious we didn't love each other, and at that point in time I don't even think we liked each other. That night, I got in and out of bed several times.

I just couldn't sleep. I kept mulling over the events of that night. Finally, after about my tenth time up, Ben turned on the light and sat up in bed.

"Are you OK?" he asked.

As I pulled the covers over my shoulders, I answered, "I'm fine."

I hated to lie, but what good would it have done to tell him the truth? How could you tell the man whose child you are carrying you made a mistake? It was much too late to do that. Lying seemed like the appropriate thing to do.

Days later when Ben came home, I didn't have dinner on the table. In fact, I had no intention of having dinner at all. He didn't talk to me as he made himself a sandwich, and I didn't care. As the hours passed, I was sure he wanted to say something to me, and it wasn't thanking me for being such a wonderful wife.

Finally, just as I was about to fall asleep, Ben turned on the light in our bedroom and lit a cigarette. He tapped me on the shoulder to see if I was asleep. I wasn't, but pretended to be. Apparently on that night he needed me, or maybe we needed each other, but it was over for me. I wasn't in love and I really didn't think he was either.

Again Ben tapped my shoulder. "Sala, I want to help you. Let me try."

After a few minutes, Ben gave up and went into the kitchen. That was when I started to cry. I had become an excellent silent crier. The last thing I needed from anyone was pity, so I kept my unhappiness to myself. I had never been one for admitting failure, but unfortunately my marriage had become just that.

All night I tossed and turned, and when I finally did fall asleep, I woke up crying and in a cold sweat. Ben ran into the bedroom and tried to comfort me, but I didn't want him to, so I pushed him away.

Trying to understand, Ben offered his help. "Sala, tell me what it is you want."

Again I brushed him away and quickly jumped up out of bed. "I don't know, but it isn't you."

With that outburst, I threw on some clothes and ran out the door, straight to Dora's.

When Dora realized I was crying, she motioned for me to follow her into the kitchen. At first, Dora didn't say anything. She put the kettle on the stove, and as she leaned back against it, she looked at me. "What's going on? Are you OK, baby?"

Emotionally, I had to let it out before I exploded. So for the first time in a very long time, I let go. "I had a dream. I saw Mother."

Dora's eyes showed concern as she poured me a cup of tea. "Mother. You had a dream about Mother?"

As I nodded my head, I could sense Dora's unease.

"Sala what really happened tonight?"

"Nothing happened tonight. I just saw mother. There was big black caravan." By this time my eyes were filled with tears. "I was dead and my baby girl was dead too."

I could feel my body shaking from within as I finished the story. For a moment or two, Dora just looked at me with a big grin on her face.

"Dora, my G-d. Why are you smiling? I'm sitting here pouring my heart out to you and you're smiling. Why?"

"Because what you're having is not a nightmare but a good dream. What you are dreaming of means you will live, not die. Mother will go for you. Mother has transferred her thoughts to you. Your daughter will live. Trust me. You'll see mother will live on through your baby. She wants to, so let her."

By this time Dora had me totally confused. "How do you know all this?" I asked, hoping for a better explanation.

Dora's answer was very direct, "I just do."

As always, I accepted Dora's words as being righteous.

Toward the end of my pregnancy, I couldn't sleep very well. I had stopped having dreams about my mother and on the nights that I did fall off to sleep, I had nightmares. Every nightmare was about the camps. Sometimes when I would wake, I could smell the burning bodies and see dead bodies surrounding me on the train.

I used to wonder when I would start to forget the horrible things I saw at the camps. It wasn't long before I realized I never would. I couldn't. Bergen Belsen was a part of my life that remains indelible, as then, now and forever.

Then came the day. I was having labor pains and didn't realize the best day of my life was quite near. Ben happened to be home that day, so he took me to the hospital. And for the first time in a long while, we were cordial to each other.

In the delivery room, I can remember looking up to G-d and silently praying, "Dear G-d, please let me do this right."

I most certainly did it right. I had a beautiful little girl. We named her Evelyn, and for a moment or two when I glanced over at Ben holding our daughter, I felt remotely close to him.

Dora was wonderful She was there when I needed her and quiet when I didn't. Once again, she had proven to me that life without her would be impossible. The doctors worried about my continual weakness and lack of energy.

Dora insisted it was because I wasn't eating, so she took it upon herself to hold a continual guard over me. She sat beside me and fed me with a spoon. She wouldn't take no for an answer.

"Eat, my child," she would say. "You need your strength. You've got a baby girl who needs you."

Dora was very right, but unsuccessful in her endeavors. I couldn't bear to eat more than a few spoonfuls no matter how forceful she was, and she could be very forceful. However, even as I grew weaker, the only thing that did bring me joy was seeing my little girl, Evelyn. Whenever I looked into her sweet, little, innocent eyes I knew I had a reason to live. Certainly reason enough to eat, get well and get out of the hospital.

I wasn't feeling as well as I pretended to be, but I wanted to go home, so I did whatever was necessary to make it possible. If it meant smiling when

I didn't feel like it or eating when I wasn't the least bit hungry, I did it. For a while I fooled everyone, including Dora, which was quite difficult. The doctors did finally agree to let me go, but not without an argument.

As the days and nights passed, I assured myself that my ill heath was due to my insistence to breastfeed Evelyn. Despite my doubts and fears, Evelyn seemed to be getting sufficient feedings. She was gaining weight, healthy and seemingly happy. On the other hand, I couldn't seem to regain my strength and the frequent bouts of laryngitis were becoming quite severe.

As the days passed into weeks, I was silently concerned as to why I was not feeling like myself. I didn't tell anyone about my fears, even Dora, but she knew me better than anyone else.

"OK, enough is enough," Dora said as she focused on my ill heath. "I've made an appointment for you at the doctor, so don't even try to argue. There is no room for discussion."

I didn't argue with Dora, but I did argue with the doctor after he told me the only relief I would have is if I had my tonsils taken out.

"No surgery for me," I said. "It's just not possible. I have a daughter who needs me."

The doctor looked at me quite seriously and said, "You won't get better without an operation. Believe me, you need this."

Dora smiled as she attempted to reassure me. "Don't worry about a thing. Irving and I will look after Evelyn."

Because of Dora's promise, I agreed to have surgery.

The operation went very well, but instead of getting stronger, I was growing weaker. My husband Ben didn't seem to notice my deteriorating condition, but Dora did. Does a mother know her child? Well, that's how Dora knew me.

On the days when I didn't even feel like getting out of bed, Dora came to my rescue. She took care of Evelyn, and for that I was very grateful. There was one thing that never changed regardless of the circumstances — I was glad Dora was on my side.

Dora kept insisting I see the doctor, but I kept hoping it was only a matter of time before I recovered completely. I tried my best to go on with my life as if nothing was wrong. But I was only fooling myself, especially when even the simplest of tasks seemed difficult.

In the quiet of the evening hours was when I began to worry about my heath. I tried my best to put up a good front during the day, but when night came, it became increasingly difficult to hide from myself.

The coughing didn't stop. In fact, day by day, I was getting worse. Once again, Dora took charge. After my visit to the doctor, there were endless blood tests and X-rays. It was all so frightening. When the doctors called me in for my evaluation, from the look on their faces words weren't necessary. Some things you just know.

The doctors' diagnosis of my debilitating cough was tuberculosis. As it would be necessary for me to have constant care, the word sanitarium bellowed in my ears. I felt as if a death sentence had been given to me.

At first I cried, but then I got mad. I really didn't understand how this could have happened, but nevertheless it had, and I was devastated. How could Evelyn be without her mommy? How would I feel without her sweet smile greeting me every day? All questions with no answers.

The doctors explained my situation to me, but instead of listening all I kept thinking about was leaving Evelyn. Bad luck seemed to follow me.

One Last Breath

Even though the sanitarium was far from Golsa, Dora managed to visit and care for me every day; nothing could stop her determination. She sat at my bedside and with the patience of a saint, Dora literally spoon fed me my meals. Never would there be anyone who would love me as she did.

And what a doctor I had. Dr. Mineheart was one terrific guy. He gave of himself, two hundred percent. Not only was he extremely competent, he was kind. There were many nights when I just needed a friend, which he was. He would sit on a chair next to my bed and talk to me about any subject I chose, listening to my every word.

He would bring me food to fatten me up, but that was impossible. As the days went on, I was getting thinner and thinner, weaker and weaker. Food wasn't appealing to me but I tried my best to eat what I could, realizing I needed my strength.

There were days when I slept like a baby and then there were days when my eyes never closed. Sometimes I was hot with a fever and other days I was freezing cold. I was more dead than alive.

I became homesick quite often, but the nurses, who were wonderful nuns, tried to comfort me. They also saw to it that each day I was taken out onto the balcony to breathe in plenty of fresh air, an important part of the healing process. When it became colder than I could handle, the sisters covered me with blankets.

Most days all I could think about was my sweet Evelyn, and how very much I missed her. I asked to see her, but the doctors wouldn't permit it. I begged for a peek, if only for a moment, but still the answer was no. The logical part of my brain understood, but my emotions couldn't stand the pain of waiting.

On the days when I felt stronger and more inquisitive, I would bombard Dora with questions about Evelyn. Do you think she misses me? Do you think she's going to forget me? Has she done anything cute or funny lately? Has she been eating? Is she still so beautiful?"

Dora's answer was always the same. "She's perfect."

Then of course there was Ben, another issue not likely to change. He was a good man, but not someone who could care for his daughter in the right way. He may have had all the greatest of intentions, but he was busy working, trying to earn a living.

For me, time passed slowly. I wasn't feeling as I should and it appeared that my strength was not returning. Then the horrible truth was discovered. I needed to have a procedure called Pneumothorax preformed on me. I was scheduled for surgery the next morning, so at least I didn't have days to agonize over the doctors' decision to operate.

When I awoke I saw Dr Mineheart, the surgeon and my family, including Ben, staring down at me. They didn't realize I was awake and I didn't let on that I was. They were discussing my heath and planning my future without me. It was as if I was dead but my spirit was there to listen. Immediately, I started to cry.

When Dora saw how upset I had become, she cleared everyone out of my room and sat at my bedside, stroking my head and singing the sweet songs my mother had sung to me. My mother was somewhere in that room. For a moment or two, I wasn't sure if it was Dora or my mother who sat wiping my clammy forehead.

The procedure had been delicate but necessary. The doctors had to collapse my lung and insert needles into my chest for air to pass through. I wasn't all the way under the anesthesia because it was important for me to be able to breathe when the doctors needed my assistance. It wasn't a pleasant experience, but certainly important to my future well-being.

The entire time I laid on that operating table, my thoughts were of my daughter. Would I ever be well enough to go home to her? And when I did would I be able to take care of her? I felt weak and unsure of my future. I do remember thinking if I was lucky enough to go home, I was never going to be afraid of anything ever again.

Suddenly, as I lay there, I could smell the burning. They said they had to burn the scar tissue from my lung. Then it began — my lung was opened and they started burning. I had lived through so much during the war I couldn't help but wonder, why now? How can I survive this illness without losing the family I love?

My body was on fire. It was my turn. I was going to die. Everything I had been through flashed through my mind. All at once, my body began to quiver from within. The burning bodies, the freshness of the memories was overwhelming to me. In my dreams I could smell the burning of others' skin. Now it was my skin, I was on fire. Then it was over. The operation ended and for the next several hours, I remembered nothing.

Hours later in the recovery room, the doctors stood at my bedside staring at me. When they didn't speak, I looked at them and asked, "Am I well?"

"Not yet," my doctor answered, as he sat beside me with this fatherly concern written on his face. "We have to keep you here a little while longer."

"What for?" I asked, quite upset with his answer.

"Sala, you need to have several treatments before we can release you. You're just not ready to go home."

"Please, Doctor. My daughter needs me," I pleaded.

"Your daughter needs you to be well," the surgeon added as he took my hand and gave it a sympathetic squeeze. "Please give it some time. You have to try to understand our concern. You have to be free and clear of tuberculosis for me to sign you out. Please be patient. It's for your own good."

"For my good, I would be out of here and with my Evelyn," I added.

Any pain that I had wasn't nearly as persistent as the constant fear of Evelyn not remembering me. She was less than three years old when all of this took place. Missing all her firsts was what hurt me the most.

When I was feeling better and days away from going home, Evelyn came to visit me. The evening before she came to the sanitarium, I didn't sleep a wink. I should have been exhausted that afternoon, but I wasn't. I was far too excited to be able to place my arms around my little girl and tell her I loved her.

Our visit didn't exactly happen as I had imagined. As I was walking down the stairs, I overheard my Evelyn whisper to my sister, "Momma, should I go to her?"

Instead of tears of joy, I felt pangs of anger. Had I heard what I thought I did? Oh boy, did I. As Dora's eyes met mine, she knew I had heard.

Quickly, Dora ran toward Evelyn and pointed toward me. "Honey, that's your momma. Go to her."

Evelyn did just that. She came to me with open arms, probably because Dora told her to. We hugged for the longest time. Right at that moment, I knew Evelyn would never make that mistake again. Just as soon as I finished all my treatments, I was going home. Enough was enough. Evelyn needed me, but more importantly, I needed her.

There was nothing I could do to convince the doctors to let me go home. Even eating meals when I wasn't hungry and sleeping as much as possible didn't ensure my discharge. A clear X-ray would have.

Finally, the day came. It was early morning, shortly after breakfast, when one of the sisters entered my room with a smile on her face and carrying a dress on a hanger.

"Today's the day. Your sister Dora will be here in just a little while to take you home. I hope you like the color," the sister said as she sat down beside me.

As I reached over for the dress excitedly, I said, "It's perfect. The dress, the day, everything."

" I should hope it is," Dr. Mineheart said as he walked in my room. "And I must say it's great to see a smile on your face."

I walked over to him and gave him a great big hug. "And I owe it all to you," I told him.

"Sala , that's not exactly true. You owe it to yourself. You're quite a fighter. You fought a tough battle, but you came around."

" I did what I had to. I always do, and I always will."

Leaving the hospital was quite a transition, but I was happier than I'd been in the longest time. I was going home to my daughter. What could be better? Even though I was still quite weak, being at home with my family and friends was the best medicine possible. I knew I had a long road back, but I was ready. For the most part, the doctors had done what they could for me. My recuperation would take time, along with several outpatient treatments, but I would recover. When they told me the rest was up to me, I knew it could be done.

America

Most of the people I knew were planning to go to America. Patiently, most waited for their papers and when they finally received them, they left as fast as humanly possible. I couldn't go anywhere until I received a clean bill of health. There was no choice. Anyone sick stayed behind.

Dora and Irving were among the first to get their papers for America. The rest of our relatives were going to go to Canada. Once you got your papers you left, that was just the way it was. No looking back, just ahead.

Within a matter of weeks, Dora and Irving were on their way to America, and my brothers and their wives were on their way to Canada. We all promised to visit each other — after all, we were a special family. We were survivors. Whatever happened in our lives, we had that common bond, a bond of unconditional love that would never be broken, even with the test of time. We may have lost many members of our family, but the love remaining for each other could never be taken away. Never.

When Dora and Irving left, we never said goodbye. We decided "see you soon" was far more optimistic, so that's how we left it. With a kiss and a hug, we parted. I had promised not to cry, but from the very moment Dora and Irving left, I found it impossible not to cry every time I thought of them. As one would imagine, I was more than lonely. I was devastated.

As the days and nights quickly passed, I had begun to wonder if my lungs would heal enough to get me to America. Strange as it seems, having a clean X-ray was probably the most important thing one could have. When you were in a public place and coughed, you were immediately whisked out of wherever you were and asked to show your X-rays. Somewhere in between this mess, I hoped for that ray of sunshine that would change my course in the direction of America.

Finally, that very special day came to be, and our papers arrived. Ben, Evelyn and I would be leaving for America in three days, probably the longest three days we would ever know. Luck played into our hand — my dream for my daughter had always been for her to be educated in the United States of America, and my prayers had been answered. Evelyn, who was just about ready to start school, was luckier than she'll probably ever realize. America was the place to be, it was going to be our home. I was certain G-d had been watching us and answering our prayers.

As the boat danced across the water, I never doubted our decision for a split second. America was where all our dreams would be fulfilled. It was our chance to change our luck and begin the rest of our lives. What a glorious feeling that was. Except for the bouncing and the vomiting, all things seemed to be going as planned. We weren't exactly on a luxurious cruise liner — in fact, it was far worse than we had imagined. Every time the boat swayed, so did I. I spent more time throwing up than anything else. Strange as it would seem, Evelyn was taking care of me. Every time I swayed, Evelyn got the wet rag out and blotted my face. It was on our trip to America that I realized I had done something right. I had been blessed with a wonderful daughter.

I don't remember just how long it took to get to New York City, but when I caught a glimpse of the Statue of Liberty, the nausea faded and my heart began to beat fast. I took a deep breath, looked at Evelyn and said, "Well my child, we made it. Here we are in America. Now our lives begin."

As the boat docked, there were several organizations with sponsors to help us with the many transitions we would face, beginning with our sleeping and food accommodations. There was a mixture of turmoil and excitement in the air but, to me, just standing there looking out at the water and feeling free as a bird was as incredible as life gets.

Changes

It was amazing how many things were happening at once. Shortly after we arrived, we were sent by train to Detroit on behalf of a very generous Jewish organization to begin our new life. We were given a check and a helping hand to get us started. Ben also had help finding a job, which certainly made things easier. However, when we had time to stop and reflect, we were not happy with each other.

Maybe it was the difficulty we had adjusting to our new lives, or just trying desperately to put the past behind us, but Ben and I were not a match made in heaven. We tried to understand each other, but we just couldn't. Maybe in some other time or place, but unfortunately our marriage was in more than trouble. It was over.

It wasn't what Ben wanted, but he knew I had to follow my dream. So when we decided to call it quits, there was nothing left to say. Ben went to live in Canada, where his family was, and I stayed in Detroit. Life felt good again. I had my dreams to get me through the rough days and the memories to make me appreciate all the good things that were going to happen. Change is good.

Detroit was warmer than we were used to, but Evelyn and I learned the place to be when the heat was powerful was the beach. So on the hottest day of the year, we put on our bathing suits and went down to the beach. At first I wasn't exactly sure what everyone did at the beach, but in several minutes we knew you either swam or sat on a blanket and looked beautiful. Naturally, I sat down on the blanket waiting for someone to discover me.

Once I realized we weren't in Hollywood, I loosened up and started to enjoy myself.

It might sound strange, and of course it was strange — I didn't really know how to have fun. At first Evelyn and I watched the others, who were sipping Cokes, playing volleyball and making sand castles. Evelyn started to walk away and immediately, I called out to her, "Be careful."

She glanced back at me and smiled. I didn't take my eyes off her for even a minute. So there I sat on my blanket, wearing large hoop earrings, high-heeled click shoes. My long dark hair was draped down my neck and my face was perfectly made up — not your average day-at-the-beach outfit.

Evelyn ran back toward me, "Is it OK if I go in the water with the other kids?" she asked.

At first I gave her a look of confusion. "Whatever for?"

Evelyn starred at me bright-eyed. "To have fun."

I nodded my head in agreement, realizing just how much Evelyn wanted to join them. "Be careful, and don't go far out. And don't talk to anyone."

I had just put on my sunglasses and a little bit of lotion when, out of the blue, this very attractive woman walked toward me holding a pencil and paper.

"Who are you?" she asked, as she handed me a piece of paper. "Can I have your autograph? I know you're a movie star, I just don't know your name."

"I'm afraid you've made a mistake," I answered. "I'm not from Hollywood."

"Well you should be," she said, as she held out her hand for a handshake. "Oh well, let me introduce myself. I'm Rita."

I immediately liked her style. "Hi. I'm Sala."

Rita put her hands on her hips and smiled. "Well now that we've straightened that out, nice to meet you."

What was funny about our meeting is that from the moment we spoke, we were like family. That had never happened to me before, but then again, I had never met anyone as genuine as Rita. We were at the beginning of a friendship that would last a lifetime.

"Have you always lived here?" I asked, wanting to know everything about her.

"No, I'm from Poland."

My eyes widened. "You're kidding?"

Rita smiled. "Who would kid about a thing like that? And you, where are you from?"

I smiled and said, "Same place as you. And I 'm not kidding, either."

My life was changing faster than I imagined. I had the opportunity to make my own decisions and I was doing just that. I felt as if I was growing up right before my very eyes. Everything I had always wanted to do seemed possible — modeling, singing, whatever. I knew it was going to take a lot of time and it wasn't going to be easy, but I didn't care. I had time and a very good friend, and life was taking on a new meaning for me, especially after Rita and I had one of her friend-to-friend conversations.

Rita blurted out, "Why are you so damn stubborn?"

"Stubborn," I shouted back. "Me? I am not."

"Yes, you are. Otherwise you'd be on the telephone trying to get yourself an interview. They're always looking for models. You're beautiful and talented. You've got it all."

I looked at Rita. "Except time. What about Evelyn?"

Rita took hold of my hand and said, "What about her?"

"I just can't leave her alone."

"You're right. So leave her with me. Please let me help."

I shrugged my shoulders. "It's not that I don't appreciate your kindness, but the timing just isn't right."

"Oh, but it is. Come on, let me help," Rita begged.

"OK," I answered. "I admit I could use the help."

Rita smiled from ear to ear. "First we've got to get some pictures of you."

After the photographs, there were the interviews. After the interviews, there were callbacks, and after the callbacks there were several offers. I had imagined myself modeling, but I had never dreamed of such beautiful fashions. They were exquisite and very fashionable. I couldn't have been happier.

When I looked at myself in the mirror, I couldn't believe it was me. I had an opportunity to wear the most fabulous fabrics and designs in department store windows. At that time, that was a very favored career. I was on my way and I couldn't have been happier. Evelyn had started school and my life was slowly falling into place.

Every time Dora called me, she was thankful that I had found such a wonderful friend in Rita. Rita helped me on holidays and weekends, and as the days passed, Rita and I became inseparable. She did for me and I did for her. She helped me with Evelyn just the way Dora had always done. I had been so lucky. I had found another Dora.

As any model knows, her time is not her own, especially when it came to getting ready for a show. I had been chosen to do a very special event, and I was hurriedly getting dressed when the designer danced toward me. I was half undressed when he neared me.

"Well aren't you a darling one?" he said with a grin.

Immediately, I reached for my robe. "Couldn't you knock first?" I asked in a slightly sarcastic tone.

The designer's voice peaked higher than mine. "Hon, I 'm not looking at you, I'm looking at my clothes. Got it babe? You better get yourself a much easier attitude, if you want to stay in the business. It's not about you. More than likely it's about me."

There was so much to learn about the business, but I was determined to know it all. I had planned to be one of the most successful models and I didn't mind working for it, so work was what I did. Day and night I worked harder than hard, trying my damnedest to get the most experience I could, realizing to be the best you had to learn it all. I was willing and able. There were endless conventions, commercials, even television shows, which I really enjoyed. It was so much like Hollywood, I was thrilled to be a part of it all.

However, there was sometimes an offensive employer who overstepped his bounds. I was in the process of learning my lines for a commercial when the gentleman, or at least I thought that was what he was, approached me.

"Are you ready?" he asked.

I turned toward him and asked, "Would it be OK if I brought my notes with me to the set just in case I forget a word or two?"

"Either you know it or you don't," was his crude reply.

I went on the set without my notes and never made one mistake, which made me, and apparently the announcer, quite proud.

"Great job," he said as we walked off the set. "How about dinner at my place? Shall we say eight?"

I looked right smack into his eyes and answered. "I'm here to work, not to play."

From that day forward, whenever we worked together, he never bothered me. In fact, he never spoke to me again, but that was OK. I was there to work, nothing more.

Then there were conventioneers and their bosses. I was asked to do a convention and, as all of them were considered noisy and hectic, I had to be in the right frame of mind. After agreeing to do one, I walked into my new employer's office and it wasn't a matter of seconds until I felt his eyes undressing me. I was uncomfortable, but I wanted the job, so I tried to overlook his vulgarity.

"I like your looks," he said, as he motioned for me to turn around. "How are your legs?"

I responded quickly. "Good. There haven't been any complaints, but if you're looking for Marlene Deitrich's legs, mine aren't."

Right after that remark he was curious, so he got up and walked around me in a circle. He looked at me and smiled. "You're hired."

There were others who were genuine and willing to give me the hours I needed to work around Evelyn's school schedule. I loved modeling and the glamour of it all, but I loved my daughter Evelyn so much more. At first she wasn't suffering, but later I could see she needed a full-time mother. I was torn between the money and the success of it all and what was best for everyone. I was a single woman with a blueprint, but in the early fifties that wasn't an easy issue. Mothering first, career second — at least that was what was expected of me.

I knew Evelyn needed to be part of a real family, so I decided we should leave Detroit and go to Chicago to be with Dora and Irving. I realized leaving Rita would be just as hard for me as it was when Dora and Irving left for America, but it was time.

Rita was quite shocked when I began the conversation. "Rita, you're great and I love you for it, but it's time for me to move on."

"Sala, why? You're happy here, aren't you?"

"Yes, but there's more."

With a warm smile Rita asked, "It's Dora, isn't it?"

I nodded, not surprised Rita knew what I felt. That's what makes a strong friendship, the unspoken words.

Dora and Irving

When Evelyn and I arrived at the train station, Irving and Dora were waiting for us with open arms. When I looked at the two of them teary-eyed and smiling, I knew I had made the right decision. They needed us as much as we needed them. I felt remarkably safe. There stood the two most precious people I had ever known. Dora was just like a mother to me, as Irving was just like a father. Evelyn was too young to realize just how lucky she was, but I wasn't. They were so genuine. With them in my corner I couldn't help but succeed.

Tears came rolling down my cheek, as Dora took hold of me and hugged me so tight I could barely breathe. "My child," she said. "I'm so sorry about your marriage. I had hoped you would know the same love I do. We didn't know. We're so sorry."

While Dora hugged me, Evelyn ran into Irving's arms. "Am I glad to see you two," Irving said as he held onto Evelyn. "We missed you."

"We missed you too," I said, as I took hold of Irving's hand.

"Sala, I 'm so sorry about Ben. I had no idea."

I placed my finger on Irving's lips. "Not another word," I said. "You meant well, I know that. Don't worry, Irving. I'm OK about it. Really I am. Evelyn and I do just fine."

When we arrived at Dora and Irving's apartment, I couldn't help but wonder how this neighborhood had gotten so mixed. It was quite a melting pot, but then again, that's what I had heard about Chicago. It was going to be a great learning experience for both Evelyn and myself. The uneasiness

I had experienced had disappeared. Oddly enough, I felt as if I was home. Actually, I was home.

I didn't want to get to comfortable living with Irving and Dora, but they were so good to Evelyn and I, we couldn't help but enjoy being there. I had definitely planned to get an apartment for us, but Irving wouldn't hear of it.

"What will people say? A young woman and child living alone, in such a big city?" Irving asked.

"People will think I'm an independent woman," was my response.

And Dora's response was, "You can be an independent woman and still live with us. There's no rule about living alone. Sooner or later we were going to look for a bigger apartment, and now we have a reason to."

Neither Dora nor Irving would accept no for an answer, so I agreed. I knew most of my energy would be taken up as I pounded the pavement looking for a job. After each interview, I wondered what I could have been thinking of when I decided to leave the established career I had in Detroit.

Finally, after several days of non-stop job hunting, Irving sat me down as any father would. "So what did you accomplish other than sore feet? Why don't you just go out and get a regular paying job?"

In my usual upbeat way I responded, "I was established in Detroit. I'll get established here."

Irving sweetly added, "Chicago's a big city. I just don't want you to get hurt."

With confidence I said, "Don't worry. You'll see, tomorrow will be better."

And that very next day, I found a job. It wasn't exactly the way I had imagined, but that's what made life such a challenge. It was after six when I finished my last interview. I looked at my prospective employer, the store manager of one of the finest department stores in Chicago, and said, "Look, I need a job and you're looking for a model. So why don't you just say yes and I'll start whenever you want me to?"

He looked at me and asked, "Where do you live?"

Not certain why he was asking, I couldn't help but question him. "What on earth difference does it matter where I live?"

With the utmost frankness, he glared at me. "I have an apartment with plenty of room for a beautiful young woman such as yourself. What do you say? "

I had suddenly become both angered and impatient. "Do I have this job or not? I came here for work, not sex. I'm a good model who's looking for an honest day's pay. You won't be sorry if you hire me."

The man looked at me as if I had just recited the pledge of allegiance. "Well I must admit you have guts. I respect you for your honesty. You're a very beautiful young woman who appears to know where she's going. You can't blame a guy for trying, can you?"

"Well, now that we've gotten that out of the way, do I have a job or not? It's getting late and I have to be on my way. So do I or don't I?"

There was a long silent pause before he spoke. "When you can you start?"

Starting Over

I guess I should have realized starting over wasn't going to be quite that easy. Every time I looked at my boss, I knew he was undressing me and I didn't like it one bit. Of course, it wasn't only me who felt like that; it was all of the girls. Eventually, I got up the courage to quit, but this time I had replaced my job with another, one lesson well learned.

While I was busy trying to make a name for myself in the fashion industry, I was extremely fortunate to have Dora taking care of my Evelyn. It was certainly a wonderful feeling not to have to worry about her. I knew firsthand how terrific Dora was at raising children. After all, she raised me.

I hadn't realized just how time-consuming modeling could be if you have a lot of bookings. The more I improved, the more responsibility my employers gave me. The one drawback was traveling. I took most of the bookings, which took me on the road a lot. I worked for some of the largest lingerie companies and was treated fabulously by them. I was earning a good living doing what I liked to do best. How much better could it get?

Well it did. I was not only doing lingerie modeling, I had started to do Ready To Ware. I was meeting buyers, having dinners, going to parties — everything was going along better than I had ever imagined. I had an agent, but I seemed to have much better luck when I did my own bargaining. My career was skyrocketing. I was gaining popularity in the modeling field, making new acquaintances and really enjoying my work. Life was wonderful and I was having one terrific time.

I began to do more runway shows than I had ever thought possible.

Along with the jobs came the dinners, and along with the dinners came the food. One night, several of the girls went out to eat. The girls had never eaten with me and as I bit into a large piece of french bread topped with butter, they sat there staring at me.

"What's wrong?" I asked, as I couldn't help but begin to feel very self-conscious.

One of the models laughed as she watched. "How in the world can you eat like that? If I so much as look at a wad of butter, the pounds land right on my thighs. What's your secret?"

"No secret. I just eat whatever I want whenever. Can't you?"

"No way," she answered, drooling as she watched me finish my bread.

That night when I went home, I couldn't stop thinking about how I could eat what I wanted whenever I was hungry and how jealous the other girls seemed as they watched me eat. They didn't know that in the camps, if I had in a total of one whole piece of bread a week, that was celebrating, let alone with butter on it.

America was the grandest place to be. There certainly is truth in the statement America is the place to live — the land of opportunity, the country of love, the place where if you work you can earn a nice living. It was all too impossible to believe how different everything was for me in the camps. No one could ever understand the pain of remembering, nor would they understand the sweetness of America and all it had to offer, if they had never been in those horrible camps. I couldn't possibly forget the pain I suffered, but I was learning how to enjoy life and all it had to offer.

However, there were still days when I couldn't seem to think about anything other than the camps and how horrifying it was to have grown up in one. Then there were other days, when I didn't allow myself to think about my past. I got up in the morning, went to work, ate breakfast, lunch and dinner, came home at night and went straight to bed. But once the lights were out and the apartment was still, that's when my mind wouldn't allow me to forget. I had dreams, horrible dreams. Sometimes I would even wake up in a cold sweat and Dora would be sitting beside me, reassuring me the war was over and Hitler was dead.

Evelyn seemed to be getting along just fine, especially since I had brought her a little cocker spaniel. We called her Lana. They went on long walks together and played outside. Everything seemed to be going along just fine, except for Irving. He was terrified of Lana, and instead of Irving growing to love Lana, he got worse as the days passed.

As loving and considerate as Irving had always been to Evelyn, he just couldn't seem to get used to Lana. In fact, it got so out of hand, Irving asked me to take Lana back. On one hand, I was very happy to see my Evelyn playing and having such fun with her new dog, but on the other hand, I felt horrible every time I looked at Irving's terrified face when the dog neared him or chewed up his shoes. I knew Lana was on borrowed time. One day soon, I would make Irving happy. Lana would return to the kennel she came from.

Love in All the Right Places

Once again, Dora approached me with another wonderful idea. "Sala, you remember our friends Shabby and Linda, don't you?"

Not realizing what was to come next, I said, "Of course. Nice people."

"They're having a party and they thought you'd like to come."

"What about you and Irving?"

"I don't think so. In fact, Irving and I fixed you up."

"Oh no, no date. I can't."

Dora seemed disappointed by my unenthusiastic attitude. "You'll go and you'll have fun. Surprise yourself."

I really didn't want to go, but I agreed. "OK, you win, but I'll meet him at Linda and Shabby's apartment."

"That'll be fine," Dora said as she walked out of the room.

I did love to get dressed up, so the evening had a purpose. I could wear my new black dress. I couldn't help but notice how excited Dora and Irving were for me to be going to the party. As I went into the living room to say goodnight, there sat Dora, Irving and Evelyn smiling in approval.

"Nice dress mommy," Evelyn said, as she pulled me down to kiss me goodnight. "Have fun."

Just as I pulled into the garage of Shabby and Linda's, I noticed a very handsome man pulling in behind me. I got out of my car and walked to the lobby. The young man didn't. I was a little disappointed, but I didn't know why. Usually things like that didn't seem to interest me, but somehow the man in the car did. I shrugged my shoulders, trying to forget him, but I didn't.

It took me several minutes to decide how the doorbell system worked. Once I did, I couldn't seem to find Linda and Shabby's apartment number, which frustrated me. So once again, I looked at all the numbers on the mailboxes, trying to find their name.

Out of the blue, a man's voice called out to me. "Do you need some help?"

When I turned around, I was hoping my face didn't show the delight I felt when I realized it was the very same handsome man in the garage.

"Can I help you?" he asked?

For a moment, I couldn't say one word because for the first time in my life, I was so enamored by this stranger who stood before me.

Once again he asked, "Can I help you?"

Quickly I responded, "Please do."

"What is the name of the person you're visiting?"

"The Corens," I said, as I looked down at the piece of paper Dora had given me.

The young man didn't say anything. Instead, he stood there looking into my eyes. Finally, he spoke, "Your eyes, they're very pretty. Are you French?"

Just as I was about to answer, another man walked into the lobby and the conversation stopped. Apparently, the other man who had just entered looked at me. "Aren't you Sala, Dora's sister?"

"Yes I am," I answered, not really remembering this man.

By this time, the elevator had arrived. All three of us entered the elevator, but no one spoke. When the elevator stopped at three, we all got out. I went to the left and the gorgeous man I didn't know went to the right. I was certain that young man who had such appeal to me was out of my life forever, but it wasn't more than five minutes when my name was called out to take a phone call. I hadn't even met my date yet, but I was pretty sure the call was from Evelyn, so I just picked up the phone and asked, "What's wrong?"

"Nothing," the voice on the other end said.

It wasn't Evelyn. In fact, I wasn't quite sure who it was. Then from behind, my date held out his hand to say hello and kiddingly whispered, "You just came in and you're already on the phone." I didn't appreciate his candor. In fact, he was rather annoying.

In a very sexy voice, the man on the phone spoke to me. "I've never done anything like this before, but I have to see you again. I was the man in the lobby who asked you about your eyes."

"Oh yes, I remember you."

"Well, that's a start," he added. "A good one, I'd say."

By this time, my date had started to become impatient. So I politely smiled and whispered, "I'll be right with you."

Then my handsome caller added, "I guess this isn't a very good time to talk, is it?"

"No, not really," I said.

"When can I see you?" my caller asked.

For a moment or two I didn't answer. "I don't know."

"I know this is very strange, but I feel that we should see each other again. My number is SH3-4582. Try to call me. My name is Jerry Lewis. Please promise to call me."

I didn't give him an answer, but I did write his number down just in case.

After the dance, I went straight home and woke up Dora.

Her first words were, "Are you OK?"

"I'm fine. I just need to talk to you."

"So talk. I'm listening," Dora said as she took my hand and walked me into the kitchen.

Dora stood at the kitchen counter making tea while I talked non-stop. "I met a man tonight and I can't stop thinking about him."

"So Coren's son was nice?" Dora asked.

"No, it's not Coren's son. He was nice enough, I guess, but it's not him. I met the most handsome wonderful man. He's gorgeous but he's wrong for me. He's not Jewish. I just can't get him out of my mind. He asked me to call him, but I'd better not. Isn't that what you think I should do?" I asked, certain she would agree.

There was a long silent pause, but then Dora answered, "What have you got to lose?"

I was shocked by Dora's eager response, so I called Jerry. It was easy enough, so we planned to go out on Friday night. Unfortunately, I had forgotten that Friday night was the night I was supposed to take Evelyn's dog Lana back.

I called Jerry back to cancel, but when I heard his voice, I decided one more night with the dog couldn't possibly make a difference one way or the other. But it did. Our date was quite memorable. In fact, after our first date I was surprised there were any more.

Right before Jerry came to pick me up, Evelyn and I were having a short but very dramatic conversation about her little dog. I was losing and I knew it, but I had promised Irving that the dog would be gone by the time he got back. Suddenly, it occurred to me that I had to change my wording if I was to make any leeway.

"Evelyn, listen to Mommy, hon. Listen for a minute. You know how much we love being together. Well, think about sweet little Lana. She needs to go back and see her mommy. What do you say? Anyway, she's probably tired of us and misses her mommy. Besides, she's chewed up all our shoes, gnawed on the furniture, and you know what all over the apartment. It's time."

Evelyn's large, powerful eyes connected with mine. "I'll take care of her. Please Mom, have a heart," she pleaded.

For the better part of an hour, Evelyn and I couldn't seem to come to any kind of understanding. I really tried to make her understand that Irving didn't like having the dog around. He was afraid of her and no matter how he tried, he just didn't feel comfortable with the dog and her free reign all over the apartment.

"Does any of this make sense to you?" I asked, trying to end this argument before Jerry came to pick me up. "Lana can't live here any more. Please, honey, try to understand."

When the doorbell rang, I ran into the bedroom to finish dressing while Dora answered the door. After the introductions, Evelyn was still crying. I motioned for her to meet me in the kitchen, but she refused. She always did have a mind of her own.

There I stood, wondering what I could have been thinking of when I arranged this night. As I glanced over toward Jerry, I watched as he leaned over to play with Lana. I couldn't help but like him. He seemed so gentle and full of love.

Nonchalantly, Jerry lifted the little dog up into his arms and walked toward the door. Quickly, he ran down the stairs with Lana in his arms, but Evelyn was not far behind him. I followed them down the stairs but because I was wearing very high heels, it got kind of tricky after the third or fourth step. By the time I reached the last stair, Dora was right behind me.

Evelyn cried out. "Please Mommy, one more night," she begged.

Before walking outside, Jerry stopped for a moment, turned around and called out to me. "Sala I'll be waiting for you in the car. And Evelyn, nice to meet you. Oh and Dora, next time I come by we'll talk."

Dora nodded and then smiled, confirming she was comfortable with Jerry.

Usually, that would have meant everything to me, but right at that moment I knew being a mother was going to have to come first. I took Evelyn's hand and together we walked upstairs.

By the time Dora and I got Evelyn quieted down, I really didn't feel like going out. But Jerry was waiting for me in the car, so I kissed Evelyn goodbye and dashed out.

The moment I got into Jerry's car, I broke down and cried. "I'm so sorry. This was a mistake. I should have never asked you to go through this."

Jerry reached for my hand and squeezed tightly. "This was no mistake."

After we brought sweet, little Lana back to her original owner, my heart was broken. I couldn't stop talking about it.

"It's my fault. I felt so guilty about working all the time. It was me who thought the dog would help, and it did. Evelyn was never alone. I just never expected Irving to be so upset. Usually whatever we did was fine with him, but from the moment I brought home the dog he was scared to death of this little, tiny nothing of a dog, although she did get bigger."

Immediately, Jerry pulled the car over and stopped. "I know what you need."

"And that is? " I asked.

"A drink. We're going to a favorite place of mine, if that's OK."

"I smiled at Jerry. "Whatever you say."

That night was one of the most special nights I had ever experienced. Jerry was just what the doctor ordered. He took me to a place in life I had never known. I laughed as I had never done before and, most importantly, I felt at ease. Whatever this feeling was, I thanked G-d for the opportunity to be with Jerry. He made the world seem brighter.

Trust and Honesty

Sitting across from Jerry, I couldn't help but want to know as much about him as possible. I had always been rather private, but as I listened to Jerry, he made it all sound so easy. He spoke to me openly and honestly, and I sat there interested in everything he said.

All of a sudden I interrupted, "Are you Italian?"

"No, I 'm a Jew. Does that make a difference to you?"

When I didn't respond, Jerry looked at me with shock. "Oh, so you've never gone out with a Jew before. Is that it?"

"No, that's not it. I've just never gone out with anyone like you."

"And you, you're French?"

When I started to laugh, he got a little angry.

"What's so funny?" he asked.

"You," I said with a smile. "Do I look French? Well, I'm not French. No, I certainly am not."

"Then what are you?"

"I'm a survivor from a Nazi concentration camp."

In a split second, the anger left Jerry's face. He seemed to be too shocked to speak, so I talked for a while and he listened. After Jerry dropped me off, I stayed up all night long, quietly thinking about Jerry and what a wonderful time I had that night.

Shortly after seven in the morning, I heard Dora in the kitchen. When I entered the kitchen still wearing the same clothing from the previous night, Dora seemed surprised. "You weren't out all night, were you?"

"No, but I didn't sleep a wink. I had a lot on my mind."

Dora motioned for me to sit by the table while she poured me a cup of tea. "Drink this. It will make you feel better. So tell me, how was your date?"

"It was wonderful. I had a great time. Jerry's the most wonderful man in the world. But …"

"But what?" Dora questioned.

"We got along famously. He told me about his life and I did the same."

"Sala, you talked about yourself to a total stranger."

"That's just it. I feel as if I had known Jerry all my life. It was so easy to tell him how I felt. I'm not sure he understood, but he listened. Don't you see I trusted him?"

"So why such a long face? " Dora asked.

"Because this isn't the right time for me to fall in love. I have my dreams, my career. Dora, you know what my career means to me."

"Sala, my child, there's no right time for love. Sometimes it just happens. Trust in what you feel. Our hearts know what's best for us. Just go with your feelings."

As Our Love Grows

Over the next few months, my career had taken off in Chicago just as it had in Detroit. The modeling agencies got to know me, and the manufacturers asked for me to model their new lines. I was once again a model in demand, making lots of money.

Jerry and I had been seeing each other on a steady basis, and even Evelyn began to feel comfortable with Jerry. But most of all, Dora and Irving really liked him.

My life started falling into place, and there were days when I fell asleep without having those horrible dreams of the Gestapo and the killing. Waking up to the dreams of tomorrow and putting the horror behind me was such a wonderful feeling. I had begun to live and I loved every minute of it. So much so it scared me.

One night when Jerry picked me up from a job, I had on a very dressy suit that I just loved. When Jerry asked me where we should go for dinner, I blurted out the first place that came to mind. "How about the Pump Room?"

From the look on Jerry's face, I could see that I offended him. "I can't afford the Pump Room," Jerry apologetically answered. "But someday soon we'll eat there, or better yet, someday I might have enough money to buy it for you if you want me to."

If there was ever a doubt in my mind about Jerry being the right man for me, at that moment I knew there would never be another man with such honesty and integrity who I could love more. There was so much more to

Jerry than he ever let on. Not only had he modeled, he was also a graduate of John Marshall Law School. Jerry had dreams just as I did, which was why we got along so beautifully. We didn't stand in each other's way and we gave each other the space to succeed, which is what Jerry continually did. He was an excellent businessman and land developer, especially in St Louis, where he transported himself back and forth.

When Jerry was away on business, I missed him terribly as he missed me. Our phone bill had become quite large, but that was to be expected. As the days passed, our love was growing, as was Jerry's list of accomplishments.

Then there was that very important moment. Jerry's mother Lillian was going to meet Dora, Irving and Evelyn. As Dora and Irving opened the door to their new apartment, Lillian walked in. I took a deep breath as I watched Jerry enter behind her. We smiled at each other but didn't speak. I imagined he was as nervous or more so than I was. Who could measure?

Lillian looked at me and then at her son. "Looks like I'm going to have myself a daughter-in-law."

I was stunned. Jerry and I had talked about marriage several times, but we never quite made it official. Apparently, Lillian knew something I didn't.

"Jerry, is this true?" I excitedly asked.

He nodded and I smiled, as he placed a gorgeous diamond ring on my finger. With tears of joy in my eyes I added, "Then I guess there is going to be a wedding."

Immediately, Irving took out the wine and Dora took out the glasses. In a very short time the glasses were filled and Irving made the toast. He was so wonderful. "Mazel tov to all of us, and especially to the lovely bride and the handsome groom. May you always be as happy as you are today. Amen"

Business Before Pleasure

"Business before pleasure," were the last words out of Jerry's mouth as he boarded an airplane to St. Louis. I was patient, but I missed Jerry so much when he had to work. Unfortunately, in Jerry's line of work, he had to go where the jobs were, so I kept myself very busy.

I had more modeling jobs than I could possibly handle, but I did my best to pick and choose the best opportunities. Several times when Jerry called me from St. Louis, I was out and he got angry. He had no reason to feel that was because my love for him was growing. It was true – absence does make the heart grow fonder.

Then there was that one night, a couple of weeks after he had left, when I had a late meeting and Jerry left Dora with a message. "I don't care if it's three in the morning. Please have Sala call me."

It wasn't three in the morning, but it was after midnight when I returned home from being at meetings all day. As usual, I peeked into Evelyn and my room, and then tiptoed beside her bed. I bent down to kiss her forehead, thanking G-d for giving me this wonderful child. Then I called Jerry.

Instead of hello, Jerry hurriedly asked, "Are you still wearing my ring?"

"Of course I'm wearing your ring. We're getting married aren't we?"

"Not soon enough for me. I miss you too much. I'll be home tomorrow evening at five. Meet me at Midway airport and we'll go dancing."

I stayed up half the night thinking of Jerry and our romantic evening together, which was why I arrived at the airport hours earlier. I hoped Jerry would be early, but he wasn't, so I made myself comfortable on an uncomfortable chair.

Because I was dressed formally, several of the women who worked at the airport came up to me, certain I was a movie star. Who else would be dressed in a gorgeous black lace dress with satin pumps, sitting and waiting at the airport at four in the afternoon?

I know I probably shouldn't have, but I couldn't help but brag about Jerry and how handsome he was. I was a woman very much in love, so why not? Every five minutes I glanced at my watch, hoping time would pass just a bit faster than usual.

Finally, the plane landed and I rushed outside to the gate where Jerry's plane was landing. There he was, full of mud and rapidly running my way. In a moment we were in each other's arms, and then I was covered with mud. We were quite a sight.

Jerry grasped onto my hand and we walked out of the field and inside the airport. Quickly, he apologized for his appearance. "I had no choice. It was either leave St. Louis without changing my clothes or miss my flight. I couldn't wait another minute to see you. I guess I didn't realize how damn much I love you."

I did, but I never told him that.

That night after we both changed clothes, we went out dancing. We had the time of our lives and everything finally seemed to be coming my way, especially when the combo band played our song, "Your Eyes are the Eyes of a Woman in Love." Life had become beautiful.

For the next few months, Jerry came in from St. Louis several times but it never seemed like enough time. We laughed, we kissed, we loved. We spent time with Evelyn and, thank G-d , she seemed happy. I couldn't think of spending the rest of my life with a man who didn't love my Evelyn. Happily that wasn't the case. We were going to be a family, and that made everything feel so right.

The busier Jerry got at work, the less time he could spend in Chicago. That meant fewer visits and more lonely weekends. I had decided that it might be fun if I went to visit Jerry, but Dora vetoed the idea.

"What will people think?" she asked. "You've got a reputation to uphold.

You're someone's mother. What will you tell Evelyn? You can't just run off to St. Louis."

"Oh yes I can," I argued, but I didn't. Dora had a much different attitude than I did, but I respected her wishes. When Jerry heard that I wasn't coming to visit, he decided he would come to see me. As it turned out, Jerry came down with a horrible sinus infection and couldn't fly.

I had toyed with the idea of going to Detroit, but it would have made Dora very unhappy and I wouldn't do anything to upset her. I would never hurt Dora. Without her love and caring, my life wouldn't be the same. I might not have been alive at all. I knew I was a grown woman, but I still respected Dora's wishes. That would never change.

Love Is Grand

On July 17, 1956, Jerry and I were married at Temple Shalom in Chicago.

I will never forget the joke we played on the rabbi. We were lucky that Rabbi Beanstock was available. He was such a wonderful man and, of course, a very important person in both our lives, especially Jerry's. After all, having the same rabbi officiate your Bar Mitzvah and wedding was truly very special.

Several days before the wedding, the rabbi asked to see both of us in his chambers. We did as he asked, not knowing what he wanted to discuss. He told us to sit down and bear with him while he explained some of the ways of the world that he thought we should know being an inter-faith marriage. Jerry winked at me to keep the joke going for just a few more minutes, so I did. We listened as he spoke.

"One belief is nice, but if that's not the way it works for the two of you beautiful young people, that's OK. G-d looks upon people not as Jew and Gentile but as man and woman, husband and wife, friend and lover. He will bless you regardless of your faith, so I would like you two to enjoy your love for each other and not worry because you share different beliefs. What matters is that you love each other and care for each other forever."

Jerry stood up, walked over to the rabbi and shook his hand. The rabbi did the same.

"Jerry, why have you stopped me?" the rabbi asked.

Jerry smiled. "Rabbi, Sala is a Jew."

The rabbi's eyes opened in shock. "Sala, is that true?"

I nodded my head, then I stood and gave the rabbi a handshake and a kiss. "It's an honest mistake. Years ago in Poland, that was a blessing."

Jerry then added, "I should have stopped you right away, but you were so serious on the issue of mixed marriage. I enjoyed hearing your honesty. You truly are a great man."

Modestly, the rabbi nodded his head in thanks.

Our actual wedding was quite small, just the immediate family — Jerry's mother, his aunt and uncle, Dora and Irving, and a few other relatives. The ceremony was held at Temple Shalom, and afterward Jerry planned a small dinner party for the family at the Covenant Club. The one mistake I made was not having Evelyn at our wedding. If there were anything I could have changed about my wedding day, it would have been that.

Had I ever thought about the problems that might occur at the onset of a second marriage, I would have insisted Evelyn be there. But at the time it didn't seem to be a problem. I was still very young, and I really thought the best and easiest way to introduce the adjustment of my marriage to Jerry was slow and easy. As always, I learned the easiest way is not always the best way, and rarely did simple answers work.

A leisurely honeymoon would have been great, but there wasn't time. Jerry had to return to St. Louis and continue his land developing, and I had to complete my modeling commitments in Chicago before I left. It was all so very exciting except for leaving Dora, Irving and my friends behind. I had done it before, but each time it was harder to leave what I had built.

Shortly after Evelyn returned from my brother's in Canada, we left for St. Louis. There was a wonderful goodbye party to wish us well, which Jerry had also attended. I really hated saying goodbye to Dora and Irving, but they promised to visit often. Even if they weren't planning on coming as often as they said they would, it certainly was comforting hearing their promises.

So once again, I was off to a new challenging life in St. Louis. If there was one lesson to be learned from all of this, it was your home is where your heart is. Once you've lost everything, beginning again becomes the simplest form of life. Losing my parents, brothers and sisters taught me to take nothing for granted and to be thankful for whatever life has to offer. I would never complain, because who would listen? Life changes from day to day and I learned long ago to follow the path that has been mapped out for me. It's easier to accept the highs and the lows if you don't question why.

St. Louis

I wasn't prepared for Evelyn's distress. I assumed that because Jerry loved Evelyn and Evelyn loved Jerry, that would be enough for an easy transition. It wasn't.

When Evelyn returned from my brother's, I hadn't expected her to feel hurt because she wasn't there for the celebration. Even though I tried to make her understand that we decided to have the wedding earlier than planned, she was still very confused about not being included. I even admitted to her that she was right and we made a mistake, but still she was angry.

When we arrived in St. Louis, Evelyn wasn't very happy to learn we were living in a hotel suite. She couldn't have cared less that there was maid service bringing us clean sheets and towels every single morning. On the other hand, I thought it was quite luxurious, a world of difference from Bergen Belsun. Topping that was a swimming pool with lounge chairs and water rafts. I felt like a queen, and in a way I think I was.

Jerry was very protective of me, somewhat like Dora. He had assumed after our marriage I would stay at home and always be there when he needed me, but I couldn't do that. My work was a part of me. It was who I was.

So there I was, once again in a strange city, knowing no one, not even knowing what street went where. But that didn't stop me. I set up several interviews for later that month, allowing me some time to get Evelyn enrolled in school and to help her get adjusted to her new surroundings.

Several weeks after I enrolled Evelyn in school, they called Jerry and I in for a conference. I couldn't imagine what Evelyn could have done for them to want to see us. I had never had an ounce of trouble with Evelyn before, so why now? Maybe new surroundings, or maybe she missed Dora and Irving, I didn't know. There were so many maybes.

I was up all night trying to understand what went wrong, but it wasn't anything I did. In fact, it wasn't anything like that at all. Evelyn wasn't in trouble — she didn't do anything wrong and neither did I.

As Evelyn's teacher opened her briefcase and took out a test Evelyn had taken, I asked, "So what is it?"

The teacher took off her glasses and looked at Jerry and I. "Your daughter is brilliant. She's gifted."

I had never heard that term before, so I listened as the teacher explained exactly what that meant. I took a deep breath and sat back in the chair, feeling very guilty about last night's sleeplessness.

While Jerry worked, Evelyn and I made friends with several of the people in the hotel. There was even a time when I could finally take a deep breath and feel as if Evelyn was somewhat happy. She laughed and enjoyed the company of many of the residents. Evelyn never had trouble conversing with men or woman three times her age, probably because for a youngster she was far beyond her years. After all, look where she had been.

We were like nomads, traveling to the promised land, wherever it might be. I hoped it was Chicago. We managed to find friends in St. Louis, but there was still no place like home. I missed Dora and Irving and I'm sure Evelyn did too, but we lived in St. Louis and were determined to make a go of it.

Along with determination and a helping hand from G-d, we managed to get used to St. Louis and all our hotel friends. That was especially true when Evelyn sold more Girl Scout cookies than anyone else in her troop, a definite plus for hotel living. There wasn't a single person living at the Forest Park Hotel who didn't eat one too many cookies. It was Evelyn's persuasive style that left no stone unturned. In fact, Evelyn was a top seller, putting her Girl Scout division over the top. We were off to a fairly good start.

It was time for me to begin my search for employment. It wasn't as easy as I thought it would be, but who said life was easy? Jerry was hoping that I would stop modeling completely, so it didn't bother him one bit that I was home most of the day. He enjoyed my cooking and loved to come home to a wonderfully prepared meal. I loved to cook and Jerry loved to eat, a definite match made in heaven. Any man who could gain forty pounds in one year is quite a man.

Evelyn, on the other hand, barely ate. She nibbled but didn't eat. Sometimes when I questioned her about why she never finished her soup, she would pretend to be slowly spooning the soup into her mouth. When I turned my back, she poured the soup out the window. I didn't let on, but what I did do was pour extra soup into her bowl, which she never touched.

When I was satisfied Evelyn was comfortable living in the hotel, I went back to work. My mornings were hectic but I made sure Evelyn got off to school before I left. Some days I had two shows to model for in two opposite directions, but if the agency gave me the address and told me the time, I would show up to do my work. It wasn't necessary to make anyone aware of the fact that on some days, I barely knew my name.

Everything changed when I was offered a job by *Playboy* magazine. I never got close enough to the deal to really know if I indeed gave up a chance of a lifetime. When Jerry heard about the offer, he wasn't embarrassed to speak out.

"How could you possibly even consider posing for *Playboy*? You have a daughter. What do think that would do to her?"

Once Jerry mentioned Evelyn's name in the conversation, it was over. He was right. I hadn't thought about anyone else except myself. It was such a compliment to be asked to pose. I only saw the popularity and notoriety I would receive. Everyone would finally know who I was, but as Jerry said, I was Evelyn's mother. I never did regret my decision not to model for *Playboy*.

I loved to cook and entertain. It was my greatest pleasure to be seated at a table with my family and friends and watch them eat the food I had cooked. I had several friends in the hotel that never cooked a meal. It was particularly satisfying to watch Jerry as he boasted about my cooking when we had them for dinner, especially after Jerry's earlier indecisiveness about my cooking.

It was an evening like any other when Dora and Irving invited Jerry for dinner. "Dora please teach Sala how to cook like you do," Jerry said as he dipped a small, broken-off piece of challah into the gravy.

As Dora answered, she smiled with pride. "Don't have to," she said. "Sala already knows how."

Jerry leaned back against the chair he was seated on and looked at me. "Is that true?" he asked.

I gave Dora a wink. "You'll just have to see for yourself, now won't you."

When I finally did cook a meal for Jerry, it was worth more than money could buy watching him eat my brisket and kugel, a dinner fit for a king. He barely came up for air, but after that he never questioned my cooking or my staying power. Meaning if I said I would cook, even if it was 104 degrees outside, I would do it. And I did, Matzo balls and all.

Better Late Than Never

When Jerry and I got married, we promised each other that as soon as there was time, we would take our long-awaited honeymoon. Time wasn't something that came easy to either of us. On the weekends Jerry had free, I was busy and vice versa.

Finally, one day Jerry came home from work with a wonderfully beautiful bouquet of flowers and said, "It's time."

"For what?" I asked as I carefully put the flowers in water.

"Our honeymoon. If we don't make time, there won't be any."

"What about Evelyn?" I asked.

"She's coming with. That's when we'll tell her I've started the adoption papers."

"Jerry, don't you think we should wait until you do?"

Jerry took me around and gave me a great big kiss. "I did. Pretty soon Evelyn's going to be my daughter, and I'm proud of that."

As I kissed Jerry, I could feel the sweetness from his lips after speaking those glorious words. Evelyn was a lucky girl. That weekend we left for Florida. It was the three of us — not exactly a very romantic honeymoon, but time to get to know each other. It wasn't all that easy, but somehow we managed to have fun.

Jerry and I were so used to working, it took us several days to unwind and by the time we finally did, it was almost time to go home. However, we did manage to get some sun and eat at some very exotic and interesting places. Contrary to the way in which I thought our vacation was going to

Marsha Casper Cook/as told by Sala Lewis

be, by the time we were ready to leave we were all very glad we came. Jerry and Evelyn became closer and somewhere between the time we left and the time we came back, home life was starting to fall into place.

The Best Life Has to Offer

For the next few years, our lives didn't change very much. Jerry and I worked most of the time and Evelyn went to school. We traveled to Chicago quite a bit, because I missed Dora and Irving so much. It was much easier for us to visit them than it was for them to visit us, so every few weeks we packed our bags and were on our way to Chicago.

Besides traveling back and forth to Chicago, I entertained our friends and business associates. Our hotel suite could hold several couples, but no one seemed to mind being a little bit crowded once they tasted my matzo balls. We laughed and enjoyed each other's company, but usually about midway through the evening, the same question would always be asked. "What was it like in a concentration camp?"

When Jerry wasn't around I answered freely, but when he was at my side he didn't let me answer. He would always change the subject. After a while, I understood why he didn't want to hear about my past. He hated to hear about my suffering and the pain – understandably so, but that was a part of my life I could never put aside.

Besides worrying about my memories, Jerry was also very protective of my health. He worried quite a bit about me and the fact that my lung condition might prove unhealthy if I became pregnant, because of my past lung condition. I knew he wanted a child, and so did I, but convincing him was another story. It took time but I finally did it. I delivered a baby boy, a wonderfully beautiful son, a welcome addition to the Lewis family. No one could be happier than I was, except for Jerry, of course. G-d had blessed me for the second time. We named our son Cort.

Jerry had promised me a very exciting present if I gave birth to a boy, and I did. Not thinking about Jerry's promise, I was shocked when he surprised me with a very romantic greeting card. There was a note at the bottom of the card, which read:

"To my dearest Sala,

You have brought me joy beyond compare Remember my promise. If you deliver a baby boy to me, you get a full-length mink coat, naturally, of your choice. So whenever you're ready, we will go to New York and whatever you want, it's yours.

Love You,

Jerry"

Months later, Jerry and I took a trip to New York. We hired a very capable young woman to stay with the kids and we were free spirits, if only for a day or two. Jerry had planned this trip so I could pick out my fur coat. It was fascinating and I loved every minute of it. Occasionally while I was trying on coats, I would pinch myself, not quite believing this was my life. Sometimes I felt as if I was living someone else's life.

While we were in New York, Jerry made sure I had a terrific time. We stayed at the best hotel, ate the best food and, as an added bonus, we saw a play. This was a world of difference from the day the boat docked at Ellis Island. That was when I was besieged by doctors and nurses, who were going over me and my X-rays, making certain my lung disease was not contagious.

About a week or so after we got home from New York, Jerry came home early from work, totally unlike him. He handed me a large box with a red ribbon on it. I knew what it was, but I was just as excited as if I hadn't known.

Quickly I opened the box and when I saw the breathtaking mink coat I had picked out, my eyes filled with tears. Jerry helped me put it on.

"Babe," Jerry said. "You look like a million."

As I smoothed my hands over the fur, I looked at Jerry and said, "I feel like a million."

Everything seemed to be going all too perfectly. Evelyn was thrilled about having a baby brother and she loved to help me, which I really appreciated. Sometimes late at night when there was complete quiet, I would look at my children while they slept and thank G-d for giving me such pleasure.

Just when you hope your life will stay just as it is forever, there's a change. Jerry came home and told me we were moving to Ohio. I had hoped that my life as it was would be somewhat permanent, but it wasn't going to be. I tried to imagine myself in another city, with new friends, a new job and a new apartment, but I didn't want to. Not again.

Another city meant a different school for Evelyn and a new start for my career. I had established some very fine modeling jobs in St. Louis, but a wife belongs with her husband, so of course the children and I would go. No matter what my losses were, my place was with Jerry, so once again we packed.

Ohio

There we were, in Cleveland, Ohio. I had dreamt about traveling to far-off romantic places, but Cleveland wasn't one of them. As it turned out, Jerry had found us a spacious two-flat that was perfect, now that there were four of us.

The only thing missing was Dora and Irving, as they weren't with us. Deep in my heart, I had always felt that Chicago was my home. Secretly I had wished for us to go back to Chicago, especially since that was where I met Jerry and fell in love.

I should have been used to separation from Dora and Irving, because as the years passed I always expected being apart from those I loved, meaning my brothers and sisters-in law. Canada was far, but at least we kept in touch, keeping us somewhat still the very loving family we once were back in Poland, which now felt like a million years ago. Time has a healing power, but the sadness I face each day when I look into the mirror prevails over all. I can't forget what I have missed. I can't forgive what I have lost, but I remember what I now have, and for that I am grateful, very grateful.

Immediately, Evelyn adjusted to her new school and her new friends. Surprisingly enough, she also joined a baseball league, as the pitcher no less. I was so very proud of her and her very positive attitude. She was quite a trooper, never complaining about having to start all over again. I don't think she knew how much easier she had made it for me, but she did, and I loved her even more for her ability to see what I could not.

Jerry had wanted me to stay at home, but I couldn't. It was in my blood to work, so I began the search to find a capable person to take care of Cort. It wasn't as easy as I thought it would be. After all, when Evelyn was a small child she had the most wonderful caretaker, Dora.

Finally, after weeks of interviews, I found a woman who was extremely capable of taking care of Cort, Evelyn and our loving dog, Jacque. Cort and Evelyn loved the little toy poodle Jerry had gotten for them. Jacque was treated like a member of the family. We all loved her, especially Jerry. He would take her out for walks but if it were too cold, he would put her in his pocket to protect her.

That's how Jerry was. He was extremely protective of the children and myself. Sometimes I would wish he would let me grow up, but he never did, and as time passed I was used to having his protection, as it was the same way with Dora. Sometimes it was uncanny how Dora could read between the lines of my life. She knew if I was happy or sad just by the tone of my voice, and so did Jerry.

It didn't take me long to find a reputable modeling agency and once I did, the jobs just kept on coming. Cleveland was good to me. I had more jobs than I could possibly handle, so much so that some days I had morning, afternoon and evening appointments.

I started with bridal shows, and from there I did newspaper and department stores. Then there were television commitments. I was the mainline RCA Victor girl. I had gotten so busy, I had no choice but to turn some jobs down. I was in demand and I loved every minute of my success.

However, I had a family and they needed me, so during the weekends I eliminated the amount of assignments I accepted. Jerry was happy and so was I.

We joined a wonderful country club and I met so many new, wonderful people. Several of them were extremely wealthy and willing to share their extravagances with Jerry and I, especially Renee.

For weeks Renee and her husband had tried to make plans with Jerry and I, but it was one thing after another. Either Jerry or I was working, but then one day Renee called me and said, "Enough of this. We're picking you up at eight on Saturday night and plan to be out very late. You guys are going to have the time of your lives."

Renee was right. Promptly at eight, the doorbell rang. It wasn't Renee or her husband, but their chauffeur. We hadn't been friends for very long and I really didn't know much about her. I knew I liked her but that was it.

When we got into the car, I expected to see Renee and her husband but instead there was a bottle of champagne on the seat with a note attached to it.

Jerry read it aloud. "Have a wonderful ride. See you soon. Love Renee."

And we did. The ride was smooth and very classy. Next, we were driven to the airport and told to wait just a few minutes until we boarded.

"I can't board this plane," I said to the chauffeur, who escorted us to the runway.

Then from behind, I heard a voice that sounded like Renee, so I turned around.

'Why not?" the voice called back.

I smiled as I saw Renee waving to us. She motioned for us to climb in.

I looked at Jerry and he looked at me. "What the hell," he said as he took my hand and we walked up the stairs.

In a matter of moments, we were up in the air. "Now can you tell us where we're going?" I asked.

"No need to," Renee answered as she snapped her fingers. I watched as three men came from behind the curtain. They had trays of hors d'oeuvres and drinks. It was elegant and fun. Renee was right. That evening was the most exciting night Jerry and I had ever had. The fact that we stayed in the air the entire night and were serenaded by five musicians made it all so exciting. That night was something that only happens once in a lifetime, if at all.

Not everything in Cleveland was perfect. There were some troubled times, beginning with my decision to help my friend at the Patricia Stevens Modeling Agency. I was the casting director. It was lunchtime on Friday when I decided to meet Jerry for a quick lunch and then return to finish up the assignments for the following week.

The weather was beautiful and lunch was terrific. I was feeling so lucky that nothing could ruin that day, except a driver not watching were he was going. Before I even knew what happened, our cars collided. I rushed out of the car, not realizing that was a bad idea considering they hit me.

"Are you alright?" I called out to them.

"Oh G-d," the young driver said as he got out of the car. "I have no insurance."

I didn't care whose fault it was or if they did or didn't have insurance, all I saw were two teenage students in the car and immediately they had my sympathy. As it turned out, they were not hurt and neither was I. At least that's what I thought.

Two days later, I woke up with terrible neck pain. I had a bad case of whiplash and for the next nine or ten months, I had to wear a neck brace. I was certain I would have this horrible pain for the rest of my life. But again G-d had been good to me, and the pain went away. Once again, I had another chance.

After numerous phone calls from the modeling agencies, I went back to work with more jobs than I knew what to do with. I was feeling good about my life and everything had once again begun to fall in place until one Sunday morning. While Jerry was at work, the doorbell rang.

Evelyn called out, "Mr. X is here."

I ran toward the door yelling, "Evelyn, don't let him in."

"I'm already in, Sala," Mr. X called back to me.

My heart started pounding as I looked into his eyes and said, "What the hell are you doing here?"

The man at the door was my ex-husband Ben. He was with one of Irving's best friends. I looked at the friend and asked, "Why did he come?"

Ben answered for himself. "To see my daughter."

I motioned for Evelyn and Cort to go into the other room, and luckily they did. I didn't want them involved in the conversation I was about to have.

"Ben, you've got guts. How dare you come to my house?"

Ben looked at me in a strange way. "I came to talk to my daughter."

"Can't you see she's scared? Why did you come here on Sunday? Did you know my husband is working? How dare you do this."

Ben took me aside and asked, "Can I talk to Evelyn?"

"OK, for one minute, and that's it."

I motioned for Irving's friend to stay with Ben when he talked with Evelyn. I stood close by during their conversation, but I never asked Evelyn what they talked about. All I wanted was for Ben to leave and never come back again, and that was exactly what happened.

Sometimes after bad comes good. It was only a few weeks after Ben had made his visit to us when Jerry came home with the best news of my life. We were going back to Chicago. There were no words for my joy, but there were plenty of tears of joy. I was elated, but more than that, I was thankful to G-d for answering my prayers. Once again, I would be with Dora and Irving at home in Chicago.

That night, I reminded myself of all the sleepless nights and everything that went with those restless moments of heartache and pain and wanting so desperately to forget my past. Strong is my memory of everything that took place years before, but yet I live my life with joy and thanks.

From the moment our boat pulled ashore at Ellis Island, I was a happy person. I had come to the land of promise, the land of fairness and understanding, a place where I could raise a family. I could be a Jew and people would respect me. I could walk down a street, any street, and hold my head up without being shot or beaten. I could become an American. I could live again.

There was one day in my life that could never take the place of any other. That was the day I became a U.S. citizen.

The night before I was scheduled to become a citizen, instead of sleeping my eyes refused to close. It was to be the biggest moment of my life. I had studied American history to great lengths and was very prepared to answer any questions they asked me. I was petrified, but becoming a citizen was the day I had been waiting for and dreaming of. When I became a citizen of the United States of America, I became the person I had always wanted to be.

Naturally, when my friends found out we would be going back to Chicago, they tried to persuade us to stay. But nothing they said could make me change my mind. I loved them all, but I had made up my mind if ever the chance to go back to Chicago arose, we would take it.

Before we left Cleveland, there was a surprise party for us held at the country club. My friend Renee was the one chosen to get me there. She did a good job of keeping the party a secret, which everyone thought impossible.

Realizing it would take some doing, she called me several days before.

"Sala, I know you're leaving and you're busy, but a gala party is being held at the club for a new TV show. Can you help me out and be there?"

"I don't know. I've got to pack and Jerry's working."

"Please," she pleaded. "Please. Do it for me."

"OK, I'll do it."

Needless to say, when I got to the country club Jerry was in front of the crowd as they yelled, "Surprise."

The party was as glamorous as they come and certainly the most exciting party I ever attended. Both Jerry and I were so touched by our friends' hospitality. They were all so terrific. I knew I would miss them, but we were going home.

Chicago, Our Home Town

When Jerry pulled up in front of Dora and Irving's apartment building, my eyes filled with tears. I felt as if I was home. As we walked up the stairs, Evelyn was right beside me and Jerry was holding a very sleepy Cort in his arms. When the door opened, I ran into Dora's arms and we hugged each other for the longest time.

Dora stroked my hair as she had done on that sunny day years before, when we were brought together at the work camp. "You're home," she said. "And we're glad you are."

My tears stopped. "Me too," I said as I followed my family into the apartment. How wonderful, I thought, to have a family.

Now that we were back in Chicago, I had to establish some of my own connections. I had lost touch with the marketplace, but after several weeks of observations and interviews, I relearned the ins and outs of the business. Knowing the business and getting a job were two different things, however. Wanting a job isn't enough — you have to go out and make it happen, and that's exactly what I did.

One afternoon when Jerry and I were out, we were listening to the radio when a young woman began to sing. I turned to Jerry and said, "I can do that but I can do it in different languages. Stop the car. I want to make a call."

Jerry pulled the car over and I got out to call the radio station.

I suppose I should have been nervous, but I wasn't. "Hello," I said as Dave Romane answered. "My name is Sala and I've just moved back from Cleveland. I can sing any song you like in several languages and I'd appreciate a chance to be on your show. I can do it."

He answered quickly. "And I'm sure you can, but ..."

"Just give me a chance. You won't be sorry."

Dave paused for a moment. "This is the craziest thing, but I need you to sing for me."

"When? Where? I'll be there," I said.

"Right now. I'm in a bind. To be perfectly honest with you, one of my singers is sick and I have a show to put on. So please, if you will, sing for me."

Jerry honked the horn, trying to get my attention. I waved back and motioned back to him that I would be right there.

I sang for a couple of seconds and before I finished, Dave said, "Sounds good to me."

Later we met and, believe it or not, that was my audition and the start of a wonderful run on the Dave Romane show at the International Cafe. I sang beautiful European songs, including Yiddish music. I was happy and so was he. From my very first week on his show, his ratings were boosted as high as ever, which certainly left Dave with no regrets.

Being on Dave's show certainly didn't hurt my job opportunities. I had enough jobs to keep two models busy. I was still modeling lingerie and various other lines.

I was having fun, but worrying about my children and wondering if they would resent me for working when most of the other mothers were home. There was one thing that I would have enjoyed more than anything — to have an opportunity to model with my daughter.

People say, "Be careful what you wish for because you might just get what you want." Well, that's how it was for me. My wish was to model with Evelyn, who happily modeled with me for a swimming pool advertisement. Unfortunately, Evelyn didn't enjoy modeling. Several months later, Evelyn and I modeled again, but Evelyn didn't enjoy it as I did. So after a few jobs, Evelyn gave up her modeling career, and I continued mine.

Life is Beautiful

As the years passed and we moved to the suburbs, Jerry and I were both very glad our children were getting a good education. Evelyn was in college and Cort was in the Deerfield school system.

I had never burdened my children with my sadness. I didn't really discuss my background with them, because I had tried my best to leave that part of my life behind me, which I managed to do very nicely.

However, there were times when it was necessary, such as the time Cort asked me to speak to his class at school. The topic was "The Diary of Anne Frank." The discussion was going to be about how Anne Frank and her family lived in hiding from the Nazis before being sent to Bergen Belsen.

"Are you sure you want me to do this?" I asked Cort. "It won't be easy."

"Yes, I'm sure. But can you do me a favor?" he asked.

If my son asked for a favor, he knew he would get it. "Of course. What is it?"

"Can you dress plain, like the other mothers?"

I knew what he meant, and I did as he asked.

I came to the school and talked to the children with the utmost honesty and sincerity. The children seemed very comfortable with me, as I was with them.

Right after the class was over, Cort ran out into the hall. I immediately ran after him and held him while he cried.

"Oh Mother," he said. "I had no idea of how horrible it must have been for you. I'm so sorry. You never told me."

"I know baby, I know," I said, as I held him tightly until he stopped crying.

Days later when Cort, Evelyn, Jerry and I were at a neighborhood restaurant and standing in line I saw a young boy from Cort's class tugging at his mother's sleeve. I had no idea why, until he came up to me with his mother right by his side. "Mother," he said. "I want you to meet Mrs. Lewis. She's not just Cort's mother, she's special. She's a survivor!"

Present Day

Sala has had two very great losses in the last few years since the book was originally published. Her husband, Jerry, the love of her life, and her sister, Dora. Without Dora's complete love and trust, Sala would not be here today.

As difficult as it always is, Sala is very accommodating during her speaking engagements. She shares her private life with audiences hoping to help heal the wounds of the past, especially for those who have loved ones away or may have lost their family or close friends.

Last Word

While writing Sala's story, I learned a truly significant lesson her story can only hope to teach. Whatever tragedy one must face — and unfortunately we all stand in the face of a possible tragedy — we must go on. Whatever it takes, whatever we must do, we should remind ourselves of the people who have gone before us and lived through sadness sorrow, tragedy and despair. They are here to speak to us, help us, and to teach us to love. We must learn from their love today ... tomorrow and forever. Thank you, Sala, for helping me understand how to go on, no matter what.

And a special thanks to my editor, Jeff D. Fleischer.

About the Author

Marsha Cook is an author, screenwriter, agent, consultant and radio host.

Along with *To Life,* she has written the novel *Love Changes,* the romantic comedy *It's Never Too Late,* and four children's books: *Snack Attack, The Busy Bus, No Clues, No Shoes,* and *The Magical Leaping Lizard Potion.* She has also written eleven screenplays in a range of genres.

To help other writers reach their goals, Marsha founded the literary agency Marcus Bryan & Associates in 1996, and achieved signatory status from the Writers Guild of America (WGA) within two years. Since early 2010, Marsha has hosted radio shows on Blog Talk Radio. She hosts a show about writing, "A Good Story is a Good Story" and co-hosts "What is Success?"

Marsha lives in the Chicagoland area, and her office is in Northfield.

www.ingramcontent.com/pod-product-compliance
Lightning Source LLC
Chambersburg PA
CBHW052054070526
44584CB00017B/2172